Is There a Cure for Masc

Also by Adam E. Jukes

Why Men Hate Women
Men Who Batter Women

Advance praise for *Is There a Cure for Masculinity?*

Just when you thought, as I do, that psychoanalysis has had its day and can bring no more wisdom to our understanding of ourselves, along comes Adam Jukes. I learned things from this book that I hadn't thought I needed to know. I also enjoyed it. – **Morton Schatzman** MD, psychiatrist and existential psychoanalyst, author of *Soul Murder* and *The Story of Ruth*

This work bursts with ideas and energy. What Jukes has to say about sulking is inspired! – Dr **Gwen Adshead** MB, BS, MA, MRCPsych, forensic psychiatrist and analyst, consultant psychiatrist in psychotherapy, Broadmoor Hospital

This book will provoke and instruct in equal degrees. Jukes' unique account of the vulnerable and brutal manifestations of masculinity pulls no punches. His voice is robust and forthright both in his descriptions – often very shocking – of male experience, and in his application of attachment and psychodynamic theories in making sense of that experience. He makes an unmissable contribution to the debate about the prospects for young men in our century. – Dr **Bernadette Wren**, Consultant Clinical Psychologist/Psychotherapist, Head of Psychology, Child and Family Department, The Tavistock and Portman, NHS Foundation Trust, Tavistock Centre

Is There a Cure for Masculinity?

Adam E. Jukes

FREE ASSOCIATION BOOKS

First published in Great Britain in 2010 by
FREE ASSOCIATION BOOKS
One Angel Cottages, Milespit Hill, London NW7 1RD

www.fabooks.com

A CIP record for this book is available from the British Library

ISBN 978-1-85343-209-5 pbk

This book is made from paper suitable for recycling and made from
fully managed and sustained forest sources. Logging, pulping and
manufacturing processes are expected to conform to the environmental
standards of the country of origin.

10   9   8   7   6   5   4   3   2   1

Produced for Free Association Books by Chase Publishing Services Ltd
Printed and bound in the European Union by
CPI Antony Rowe, Chippenham and Eastbourne

To my daughter Elli and my grandchildren Ben and Bea.
You're what it's all about.

The phallus serves its function best as veiled.
[If you keep your sword in its scabbard
no-one will know what size it is]

Contents

Preface

I wrote this book because I believe I have had a unique opportunity to develop a perspective on men and masculinity that is different from the usual. In fact some might say my view is idiosyncratic or iconoclastic. Because of that there are many things that this book is not about. It is not about male depression, or impotence, or relationship difficulties or aging or homosexuality. However, I hope each of those is made more understandable by what follows. I have been fortunate in having a practice which for almost 30 years has been dominated by working with male patients – something which is, if not unique, rather rare. Men are notoriously reluctant to present for the talking/feeling cure and this is more than myth. As this book will show, there are obvious reasons why men would feel very threatened by such a revealing process. I have always believed in applying theory to my work with people and the theories that have shaped both the style and the content of my work will become apparent as I proceed. However, I have always preferred my work to be practice led as far as possible. The truth is that much of who I am as both a professional and as a person (and they are not so different now) has been shaped by identifications with various important people in my life and they have also been shaped by their own. Apart from Melanie Klein, Donald Winnicott and Michael Balint there is a number of oddballs. Laura and Fritz Perls, the founders of Gestalt therapy were therapists to my Gestalt therapist, Ischa Bloomberg, and contribute to an occasional wildness in me. David Malan, Margot Waddell and Lionel Kreeger, as eminent analysts, need no further introduction. These have all gone into the mix and one way or another contributed to what I consider to be my own analytic and therapeutic voice and its catholic origins are reflected in what follows. This is not an academic or scholarly work. There are many who have addressed the issues in this book and I think my previous books have addressed the most valuable contributions. However, I want this to be accessible to the educated reader and it is written with that in mind. I may have attempted the impossible in writing a book that would be of interest and value to the general intellectual reader, with an interest in these matters, as well as the counsellor, social worker or psychotherapist. There is a risk I will satisfy neither.

Copious references can be off-putting to a reader and the idea of them was certainly so to me after the effort involved in writing what I consider to be academic work previously. I can only apologise to those who think I ought to have referenced them and to express the hope that this work will encourage its readers to carry out their own research. Also I have not broken up the text with references and as well as keeping them to a minimum have placed them in a section of chapter notes at the end of the book.

I remember being very impressed when reading Donald Meltzer's book on perversion. In the introduction he states that the book is about him. I thought it rather too self-disclosing at the time but of course it is simply a statement of the obvious. Every book is about its author, just as this is about me. Every experience and conclusion I document here are those of my patients filtered through Adam Jukes. In that sense this is a very personal book.

It will be clear to readers that I am no fan of post-modernism. One of the characteristics of my written and clinical work is that I am pretty direct. I am not uncomfortable with confusion or uncertainty but I like to do what works and, in my opinion, post modernist therapeutic thinking is of little value to people in pain. I know I will be charged with reductionism by some readers.

I am prepared for that. My fondness for modernism does not preclude nuanced or complex clinical narratives and theoretical constructions but I see little use if they merely serve to obfuscate or confuse without increasing understanding.

Acknowledgements

As usual, there are many people without whom this book would never have seen a printer. The most important are the hundreds of men who have given me the opportunity to learn to do something which I enjoy profoundly and to make a living from doing so. I hope the benefits to them were equal to mine.

The manuscript was read and commented on wisely by Bernadette Wren, Gwen Adshead, and Morty Schatzman. My son, Tom Jukes, was generous in the extreme with his time, his wisdom and his technical skills, ably supported by my favourite daughter-in-law, Sam. This is a far better book than it would have been without their generosity. Tom Evans provided his valuable help in getting us started on the design process and Graham Chweidan was more than generous with his professional photographic talents. My gratitude goes to Trevor Brown without whom the book may never have seen the light of day. My *éminence grise*, my wife Melinda provided the secure base required. Without her this would never have been written. Finally, I must also mention my daughter Elli, who once asked me 'what is masculimity?' In the family this book will always be known as 'Is there a Cure for Masculimity?'

As usual the final voice is entirely my own. Whatever its origins it speaks me and the influences which went into the melting pot of its birth but final responsibility for it remains entirely mine.

When I was a very young psychologist and trainee psychotherapist I was much attracted to any theory which was not Freudian. I was attracted to Gestalt therapy, Transactional Analysis, Neurolinguistic Programming, Hypnotherapy, Bio-energetics and encounter therapy. Not that I was ignorant of Freud, on the contrary. In fact it was psycho-analysis that eventually guided me out of all the various traps I got myself into in my efforts to avoid doing what I suspected was the right thing – to get myself into analysis. However, during my somewhat intellectual youth I was approached by a man for treatment and what happened was to have a profound effect on my subsequent choice of clinical interest.

This was a highly intelligent, softly spoken and rather timid man who confessed that he was unable to have sex with his wife of two years and that she was threatening to divorce him. He had become impotent soon after their marriage, having been potent during their courtship. I had made a couple of exploratory interventions only to have him rebut them rather quickly and certainly, but without aggression. I was beginning to feel quite impotent (surprise, surprise!) and after about a half hour (all we humanistic therapists wanted to 'cure' quickly in the Sixties and Seventies!) I asked him a couple of questions about his father whom he described as an abusive and terrifying bully. I rather quickly made a silent interpretation about the origins of his impotence and made a forceful intervention to the effect that I thought he was wasting my time and that so far as I could tell his impotence was probably incurable. I made a few more remarks to the effect that he should save his money and my time and give up trying to solve the problem. He was, understand-ably, angry and left the session prematurely. That was a Friday evening. On Monday morning I took a call from him asking if he could come back and see me one more time and promising that he would pay me for both sessions. I agreed to meet with him a day or so later.

What happened in that subsequent session was to lead me by the intellectual nose to what follows. In effect I began writing this book then. If you need to know now what happened in that second session you can turn to the Postscript. Otherwise you can read on and try to work out what you think the outcome might have been based on your reading of my understanding of masculinity.

1
Introduction –
Clinical Case Studies

Some everyday stories. There are quite a lot of these and that is partly because I enjoyed writing them.

A president begins an illicit affair with an intern at the White House. He is 25 years her senior. The affair is discovered and he bends and distorts the truth to the whole nation and eventually the fuss dies down with only minor damage to his reputation. He is married to a beautiful and clever woman who has given up a great deal to support him in fulfilling his ambitions.

A cabinet minister is discovered to be having an affair with an actress 20 years his junior. It emerges that apart from enjoying sucking her toes he insists on wearing the shirt of the football team he supports whilst they are making love. His wife and the mother of his three children forgives him although the disclosure of the affair by the actress costs him his career.

A male MP is found dead from asphyxiation after indulging in a perverse and dangerous form of sexual activity which involves bondage and the deprivation of air during orgasm.

The editor of an influential political magazine, an extremely intelligent man in other respects, is discovered to be having an affair with a much younger woman. The disclosure costs him advancement and maybe his career.

A very senior cabinet minister has an ongoing affair with his secretary and informs his wife in a very cruel way. He divorces her and marries the secretary without damage to his career but much shame and humiliation when his wife discloses information about his private behaviour.

A pop star is discovered to have thousands of illegal and disturbing pictures of children on his computer. He is sentenced to jail and his career is ruined. He emigrates to the far east and a year or so later is arrested for having sex with underage girls. He is sentenced to a long term of imprisonment.

An eminent psychoanalyst is accused by another psychoanalyst, who was his former training patient, of inappropriate sexual behaviour with her. It emerges that during her training he was having sex with her during the sessions. He is ejected from his institute and struck off the medical register.

A consultant gynaecologist is found guilty of sexual assault on a patient. After the allegation is made by her, many other patients come forward and report that he had done the same to them. He is struck off the medical register.

A senior MP, married with three children, is seriously assaulted by two men after he approaches them for sex in a park late at night. The subsequent revelations about his long standing and secret homosexual behaviour cost him his career.

A senior US senator denies allegations, made by a rent boy, that he has been paying for sex regularly with him. His denials are fruitless and his career is ruined. He is married and has consistently voted against any legislation which may further the rights of homosexuals.

The editor of a national newspaper is outed by a prostitute who he has been seeing regularly for some years. He is married with children. His career is not harmed by the disclosure.

A senior manager with an international IT company is discovered to have thousands of pornographic pictures of children on his company computer. He is discovered when his computer becomes so slow because of the amount of pictures stored that he has to call in the company's experts to find the problem with it. They discover the pictures and he is dismissed;

the police are called and he is charged and sentenced to three years imprisonment. His career is ruined.

A senior manager with an international food company is found to have been taking large bribes from suppliers to place contracts with them. He is dismissed and his career is destroyed. His wife eventually divorces him and gets custody of the children. He becomes a drug addict and alcoholic and it takes him many years to get his life back into order.

An immigration judge is involved as a witness in a court case brought by his cleaner, an illegal immigrant. It emerges that he has been having sex with his cleaner for many years and that he knew she was illegal. His career is damaged by the disclosure.

A prime minister who is renowned for preaching about family values has an affair with a minister and it is kept secret until she is sacked and she discloses it. He is wounded but not below the water line. Her reputation is advanced, but not as a politician.

A deputy prime minister has an affair with a junior adviser, often having sex in his office with the door open as if inviting discovery. No doubt the risk of it increased the illicit thrill. He is damaged but manages to hang on to his job. She is effectively dismissed by being sent to do a job in an outlying office which is much less demanding than her previous role. He speaks against her in public. In revenge she discloses details of their affair which are deeply embarrassing to him.

A very popular television presenter, a 'happily married' father of three, winner of all manner of awards, is discovered to enjoy taking cocaine and wearing women's underwear at sex parties which do not involve his wife. His career is ruined.

Another popular and intelligent television presenter, who enjoyed lampooning the above presenter for his proclivities, was discovered, ten years later, to enjoy taking cocaine whilst having sex with prostitutes. His career was badly damaged and may not recover.

A children's programme presenter was discovered to enjoy taking cocaine and indulging in sex parties. His career is ruined.

A famous author and politician is accused of having sex with a prostitute. He denies it in court during a libel action at which his wife also appears as a witness. He wins the case but is later discovered to have committed perjury. He is sentenced to a long term of imprisonment. His political career is ruined.

A famous, iconic footballer is disclosed to enjoy wearing his wife's underwear when he is not at home – that is, ordinarily, not during sex. His wife makes this known in a jokey interview. Many jokes are made but he seems undamaged by the revelation.

A cabinet minister is accused of taking bribes. He issues a fervent denial and sues the newspaper editor who made the allegation. He is later discovered to have perjured himself during the case and is sentenced to a long term of imprisonment. His political career is ruined.

A famous cricketer is accused by a lover of having violently attacked her. He denies the allegations which are carried in most newspapers. However, other women come forward and attest to the same thing. His reputation is in tatters and his career is badly damaged.

The former lover of a famous footballer, herself a well known television presenter, discloses that he has regularly been violent to her. His reputation is badly damaged but his career is unaffected. However, after his retirement he is not offered opportunities to be a pundit on football programmes.

A famous footballer is revealed to have been paying for sex with a prostitute who is old enough to be his grandmother. Although he becomes the butt of many jokes, and there is talk of his fiancée being very upset, his career is not damaged by the revelations.

A leading evangelical and fundamentalist Christian who campaigned against homosexual marriage and against homosexuality was discovered to have been paying for sex for many years with a male prostitute. The evangelist is married and has five children. He has close ties with the republican party and the White House. He resigns his post and his career is ruined.

A Chinese-American mathematician published an article about how a particular theory could be applied to the development of financial derivates. In the article he is particular to warn of the axioms he has used and how understanding these and taking appropriate care is essential to the adequate assessment of risk associated with any derivates developed from this model. His work is used to develop Collateralized Debt Obligations but his caveats are ignored. The world is brought to financial meltdown by the men who developed the CDO and ignored the risks he outlined as they pursued short term profit without thought of long term consequences.

A middle aged factory worker (X), who is married and has two daughters, creates an online identity as an 18 year old soldier. He begins a passionate online relationship with an 18 year old college student. They never meet but the relationship progresses to telephone contact and explicit sexual communications. The man's wife discovers the relationship and contacts the young girl by phone and discloses her husband's real identity. The young girl does not believe her so the wife gives the contact details of a friend and work colleague of X who confirms what the wife has said to her. Amazingly the young girl then begins a passionate online relationship with X's colleague. The young girl, Jessy, contacts X and discloses everything that has happened. A short while later X's friend is found shot dead. The police suspect X and, worried for the safety of the young girl, attempt to contact her. They discover that she is, in fact, a married, middle aged housewife and the mother of the 18 year old daughter whose photographs and possessions she had been sending to X. X is eventually arrested and charged with his friend's murder. His life is in complete ruins as he faces life imprisonment if found guilty. His wife comments that she had been living with a stranger since he began using the internet and that there had been no traces of the man she had known.

An oft repeated 'fact' is that as many as 40% of men are at some time violent to a female partner. Although more men are now prosecuted for this, it remains true that most are not and that 'domestic violence' (battering) is still largely denied and ignored by policy makers.

Pornography, produced by men for men is one of the world's largest and most profitable businesses. According to some research over 90% of internet traffic is pornographic. It is surely not feasible to suggest that it is viewed and used only by lonely or sexually disturbed men. In fact the available evidence suggests otherwise. It is used by 'ordinary' men for the purposes of masturbation on a regular basis. In recent years, 'Lads Mags' have taken to publicizing and rating pornographic websites for the benefit of their readers. Some of this traffic is beyond simple gynaecology, it involves women in truly grotesque situations involving animals or objects or substances, the perversity of which would make one question the sanity of any man who found such images arousing. No doubt many of these men are really disturbed. Equally, I am sure that most are not.

A very famous sport star is caught in a series of infidelities that lead to the breakdown of his marriage and the termination of some lucrative sponsorship contracts. After a while he announces that he is to return to his sport but that he will not be terminating his 'treatment'. I wondered what he was having treatment for. After all, he had spent his life perfecting his skills so that he could gain as much money, power and status as was possible and one of the main reasons for that was so that beautiful women would want to have sex with him. After finally achieving his lifelong goal he was told that he was 'ill'. What, precisely, was he being cured of? Well, of course, it was of 'being himself – a man whom millions of other men wanted to be and whom millions of women want to have sex with. This is not to deny that his behaviour might benefit from some deconstruction but, *ill*? I think not. Sexual addiction is an interesting new 'illness', a condition which seemingly afflicts only men. No doubt it provides some therapists with a good income and is a subject of much brain beating in major drug companies as they attempt to find a 'pill' for this new medical condition. Therapeutic treatment for sex addicts is 'big business' in the USA and some people are attempting to similarly establish it in Europe – 'big business' is the operative expression here.

And the point is?

I could go on and on, multiplying these examples of successful men whose identities and careers have been subverted by sex, money and violence although it is true to say that money and violence to women are less destructive to careers than is sexuality. And nothing subverts identity quite like sexuality. It is seemingly impossible to find as many examples of such identity-subverting behaviour involving prominent women. Why is this? Are these men normal? Does their behaviour reflect what we already know to be an obvious truth, that most crime, whether sexual or financial or violent, is committed by men? Could it be that public success is itself a 'cause' of these behaviours in that such men are subjected to intense scrutiny by the media and that what goes unnoticed in ordinary men is simply picked up because of the public interest in the private lives of celebrities? Should we be surprised by such behaviour? Why are careers ruined by this apparently normal behaviour? What constructions of maleness and masculinity do we hold that dictates that these men should be ruined by the disclosures mentioned?

Why is it that crime seems to be a masculine activity? Is perversion similarly a male pastime? Are these men different from other, 'normal', men who don't appear in newspapers or are not the subject of intense scrutiny by journalists? I am going to present many similar examples of 'deviant' behaviour as I hear of it every day in my consulting room. I am given many opportunities to speak at conferences and in the main the audiences I address are composed largely of women. As I talk about the men I work with and their peculiarities, whether sexual, violent or otherwise, I frequently see women nodding and smiling. Frequently they break out into loud laughter. More often than not, many of them approach me afterwards and tell me that they have never heard their husbands or partners so well described. It is also true to say that I meet with stern challenge from women and occasionally from men in such situations. They protest that I present all men as perverse or violent or otherwise behaviourally disturbed. When I take up the challenge, often the differences they tell me about are quantitative, not qualitative and, equally often, the men they have known are, apparently, more deviant than the men I work with. Some of my patients are celebrities or otherwise very successful, but in the main they are fairly 'ordinary' and not subjected to public scrutiny. Are they different from 'normal' men? I do not believe so but the reader must decide on the basis of her own experience and from her reading of this material.

Additionally, most of the men I know as friends or colleagues have a hidden self – but not so hidden they are unwilling to share it with me. When my first book, *Why Men Hate Women*,[1] was published it was suggested by one reviewer that I was either a self-hating man or a man who hates men. I feel confident in asserting that I am neither. Joyce McDougall made a plea for a measure of abnormality in the way culture and psychoanalysts and therapists see people.[2] I can only echo that plea and this book is, amongst other things, an attempt to do that.

I feel very privileged to have been allowed into the lives of the men you are soon to read about. I have taken great care to protect their identities and where possible have asked permission to write about what they disclosed to me. Surprisingly, none have said no.

I would like to state the obvious at the outset. The view of men presented here is undeniably idiosyncratic – some might say extreme. I freely acknowledge that I have inhabited a privileged position for over three decades insofar as I have been allowed access to many men's most secret and shameful fantasies and activities. That is what this book is about – the darker sides of masculinity. Uncomfortably close to the creative genius required to paint *Guernica* is the violence and destructiveness which is its subject matter. The tools required to inflict that destructiveness and suffering on its innocent victims required, for their invention and creation, levels of creativity equal to that possessed by Picasso.

This book is not only about the origins of that age-old conflict between destructiveness and creativity or love and hate but it is also about the forms in which individual men act it out in the true sense of that phrase – without insight or awareness. It is my belief that masculinity is predicated on a fissure or fault deep within the male psyche. Perhaps it would be more accurate to say that masculinity is based on a structural fault in the male psyche, that at some point in development a seismic shift occurred, similar to the action of tectonic plates shifting apart. This 'basic fault' or fissure is the resting place of psychological masculinity, a construct I shall define. On one side of that fault, the underside, is a non-gendered child, mainly relating to his primary carer/the breast whether securely or otherwise. The topside of that fault is the combination of the secret and the visible that we call a man. Men's struggles with that fault in adulthood, the conflict between the desire to embrace the underside or to eradicate it (an impossible task) are the subject matter of my everyday clinical practice. The compromises, bargains, fudges, contradictions and lies in thinking and feeling and particularly behaviour are the symptoms handed to me by my patients. This book is an attempt to explain that fault and follow the paths men take on the route to developing some sense of a stable masculine identity, or at least to one which provides the illusion of stability and the possibility that it can be managed. I have tried to make this work something different from ordinary books about men and psychotherapy. What interests me about men is the apparently deviant qualities to our nature. I attempt to show that what we think of as deviant is actually rather ordinary, or connected to the rather ordinary in obvious ways and in effect to plead for tolerance for a measure of 'ordinary deviance'.

It might help if I present what I believe to be a major milestone in establishing the bedrock of masculinity. Naturally, from my viewpoint, it concerns the penis. Early in growth I am convinced that little boys discover that fondling the penis is pleasant even if it is not accompanied by erections. From the age of about three it is so accompanied usually. It does not take long to discover that fondling it during times of stress, anxiety or undifferentiated upset, and particularly during episodes of separation anxiety, provides real relief from distress. This is the moment when masturbation registers as a major stress and anxiety coping mechanism for the little boy and fixates it for the later man.

Following this discovery and the subsequent heightened valuation of the penis there is the onset of the Oedipus complex where the boy desires to replace the father in his relations with the mother and experiences homicidal rivalry with the father. This is the so called positive complex with which we are all familiar. Opposed to the impulses it contains are the impulses associated with the negative version of the complex in which the child wishes to replace the mother in her relations with the father. The naming of these opposing trends as positive and negative reflects the normative nature of this particular Freudian theory.

The significance of the Oedipal drama is that it 'elevates' and potentiates the significance of the penis in the emerging male psyche. It comes to symbolize all that masculinity is and should be. The relationship between the 'fault' and the penis is what defines this book and many of the forms of masculinity which I meet in my practice.

I have said that this in not an academic book. By that I mean that it is not packed with references to the work of other authors who have struggled with the issues it is concerned with. The attraction of writing this book was that it offered me the opportunity to write something which I could enjoy – and I do not enjoy researching – and which primarily gave me the time to reflect on what it is I do rather than what others do. In that sense this is explicitly a highly personal work. Not that theory will be entirely absent – on the contrary. However, I want to attempt to allow it to develop from the practice examples rather than the other way around. Far too often practice is theory driven and this is a substitute for understanding, engagement and risk taking.

This book is about men. Specifically, a great deal of it is about therapeutic work with what I have come to regard as the norm for men – deviant behaviour. Such a statement will require some explanation and justification and rather than setting out a long philosophical and intellectual case for it, I will allow the text to speak for itself through casework and analysis of material.

For many years analysts and therapists have been preoccupied with men or, more specifically, masculinity. There is, of course, a difference to be made here. One of my favourite books about masculinity was written by Stephen Frosh.[3] I followed some of his ruminations and personal disclosures with my own in *Men Who Batter Women*.[4] I vividly recall both his and my own struggles to define masculinity and differentiate it from its supposed opposite, femininity. We both discovered that the harder we looked at it, the more we were stuck in a dialectic in which the opposition became more and more blurred. It has taken me some time since to realize that the dialectic is actually a dead end. If we want to know about masculinity we simply have to ask what it is that men do. Masculinity, like femininity, is a form of action – it is what men do, and that is what this book is about.

Naturally, I am obliged to consider how representative are the accounts in this book of normal masculinity or men. Ever since Freud's first book appeared, his theory has been charged with being one about abnormality as it was based entirely on 'patients'. In some respects this may be true of the content of the theory of psychoanalysis but it is a more difficult charge to sustain when considering the meta-psychology or his theory of mind. However, insofar as the ideas in this book are concerned I firmly believe that these men are representative of all men and that any differences are quantitative rather than qualitative. There is no doubt that what I do in my work with men is little different from what therapists do with women – we work to analyse transference and the unconscious. The meta-psychology remains the same. Ultimately it is for the reader to judge.

In recent years it has become fashionable to opine that men are struggling with a 'crisis of masculinity' largely as a result of the impact of feminism on women's attitudes and the changing nature of work in advanced post-industrial economies. Whilst this explicitly rules out any such crisis in the majority of the men in the world who are not living with post-industrial angst I believe this 'crisis' is chimerical – a figment of the imagination of writers for women's magazines. I have seen no such crisis in my male patients during the last 30-odd years that is expressive of any cultural shift. The dilemmas and conflicts about relationships that men presented at the beginning of my career are much the same as those presented to me today. As I will attempt to make clear, the 'big M' as I call it, is alive and well and living in Paris, Delhi and New York just as it has always done. I believe the real change has occurred in women as they have held up a mirror to men in ways which would not have been possible in the majority of the 20th century. Obviously this has required adaptations from men as they have attempted to retain the privileges, the rank, status and social esteem, of their gender without confirming the unpalatable image being reflected. As to the 'crisis of masculinity', I believe that this is transhistorical and transcultural. I see masculinity as being formed in a crisis. This crisis is the Oedipal complex and I believe the crisis underpinning the resolution of the complex is omnipresent in men. As I hope to show, the threat of the underlying anxieties breaking through is responsible for most male pathology.

I want now to illustrate different aspects of masculinity and sexuality and to outline the 'fault' and its origins. Although I am not formally an attachment therapist, I think of myself as such and it will become clear how much my work is influenced by the attachment perspective and by attachment theory.

2

Attachment, Intimacy, Separation Anxiety and the Fear of Women

The attachment disorder

This is a session with an angry man with an attachment disorder who I had been seeing three times a week for six months after some time at once weekly. He is a very intelligent and articulate businessman, but apart from anger and rage he had rarely been in contact with any feelings. However, he had made a strong commitment to treatment after being ousted by his wife. The children of course stayed with her. It was not until he lost her as a result of his rages, that he realized how much his wife meant to him. For the first time in his life he had begun to experience sadness and grief in a free floating form, but not yet any genuine remorse. Unfortunately, he had been in an alternative form of therapy for two years previously and his therapist had been of the dominant persuasion insofar as marital difficulties are concerned. In the main this is a theoretical elaboration of the belief that 'it takes two to tango'. He was a perfect example of a case I have argued elsewhere in that his abuse had become more intense and damaging during that treatment. His therapist had provided him with a theoretical underpinning for his violence. They were a 'violent couple' in which he held the violence and she the sexuality and vulnerability. As will become clear I believe this is a form of therapeutic madness.

At this point in his treatment, about six months in, he had made significant changes in his behaviour (largely as the result of some fairly intensive cognitive behavioural work we had done) and was re-united with his family and going to the family home for weekends. He was once again living in the family home although in a different part of their very large house. We had just returned from the autumn half-term break. Although we had progressed to the couch and three times weekly, I had not been making very dynamic interpretations to him. There were many reasons for this, which will become clear later in this work. He lay on the couch with a heavy sigh. As usual I said nothing. After a while he began to tell me about his young son. When he had gone home on the weekend beginning the break his son had been quite difficult. He had behaved very angrily toward his father and had rejected him in no uncertain terms. My patient was bewildered by this and had repeated his attempts to re-establish his relationship with his son. He had been repeatedly rebuffed and had finally given up. Within a short time of being around him, the boy had finally made an unsolicited approach to him and contact was finally made. My patient said how confused he had felt. He did not know why the boy was so difficult and angry but he himself had felt like retaliating and being angry with his son. He had not known what to do but had thought about being in a session with me and knew that I would have dealt with it by simply waiting it out and this was what he himself had decided to do.

He fell into silence. After a few minutes I remarked that maybe he was trying to let me know how much he had missed me but was afraid of letting me know how angry he felt with me for abandoning him in case I retaliated. This was the first transference interpretation I had made, and as these things go it was fairly mild. This highly cerebral, alexithymic (a deficiency in describing, processing or understanding emotions) man said nothing but tears were silently coursing down the side of his face. He continued to cry in this way for about three minutes before beginning to talk. Subsequent events in this man's analysis confirmed that this was the first time in his adult life he had been able to acknowledge an important attachment to another adult whilst he was in the attachment. It was also the first time he had been able to acknowledge any sadness about absence in the presence of the object which had been absent. This simple breakthrough heralded major changes in the organization of this mans' internal and external worlds.

This illustrates some of the major themes around which this work is organized. Those themes are primarily concerned with the amount of identity management (a simple definition of which is how much of the self has to be suppressed in interaction with others or to maintain a sense of one's integrity) which men are engaged in and the extent to which the male self is a construct requiring excessive amounts of suppression and repression of non-male qualities. Male violence and sexuality are also of primary importance here insofar as it is in these two areas of life that a great deal of maleness is negotiated so naturally there will be much about both here. Most of it will be what is usually passed off as perverse or deviant. However, what I hope will become clear is that what usually passes for perverse or deviant in male sexuality may be more normal than we usually allow for.

Detachment and the fear of intimacy, anxiety and vulnerability

The study above effectively lays one of the bases of my central hypothesis which I now want to tease out; that masculinity is predicated on a fault and that this fault is a consequence of loss and that this loss leads to attachment and commitment problems and to profound separation anxieties.

In my experience men are not very good at metabolizing anxiety. We know that women tend to suffer from internalizing disorders such as depression and men from externalizing disorders involving aggression, narcissism, obsessive-compulsion and paranoia. For reasons that I hope to make clear men have great difficulty with feelings and intimacy and this is because of the way we respond to shame and shame related emotions like embarrassment, humiliation and guilt. Essentially, as I will show, we are shame phobic. We tend to use reactive defences like projection, intellectualization, rationalization, reaction formation, overcompensation, grandiosity, devaluation and denigration and idealization. These are all attempts to change rather than simply suppress or repress what we experience. Little girls tend to make the masochistic move described by Janine Chasseguet Smirgel[1] whereas little boys make the move to activity (sadism?) and acting out. Part of the aim of this book is to understand why.

One anxiety it seems to me that men have particular difficulty with is separation anxiety or anxiety about loss, and men associate these particular anxieties with shame. Time after time in my professional life I have been met with complete bewilderment from men when I have ventured to suggest that the symptom they are experiencing prior to a break in treatment is a defence against the separation anxiety precipitated by the break. As I have already said, I see myself basically as an attachment therapist. What this means is that I see most problems as deriving from bad attachment experiences in childhood. Most of the men I have worked with go to some lengths to deny that their bad early experience has had any impact on their development. In effect, most men, certainly the ones I have worked with, are in a state of denial of attachment. Their dominant attachment style is detached. I realize this sounds oxymoronic but it is only apparently so. In the marital therapy literature there is much time and energy devoted to a common couple – the pursuer wife and the distancer husband (she has a preoccupied insecure attachment style to go with his detached insecure style). The dynamics of their relationship are characterized by her efforts to become intimate with him and his efforts to avoid it. It is as if they are joined together by a ten foot pole; she cannot move towards him without pushing him away. I believe I can safely say that there are very few women who have not experienced this in their relationships. I shall explore detachment in more detail later.

Female patients have little difficulty, in general, in connecting their anxiety with breaks in treatment. Consequently, acting out tends to be relatively circumscribed with depressive symptoms prevalent. Men are inclined to act. They get angry with people who let them down or who do not serve them well, particularly their partners; they feel agitated, drink, gamble, visit prostitutes, use pornography and often masturbate to excess. It can take many repeated separations before it finally becomes clear to them that this escalation usually happens prior to and after breaks. Once that connection is established, valuable work in the transference can begin (the transference is when the patient sees and reacts to the therapist as if he is someone from his past, usually mother or father). The inability of a patient to acknowledge the connection, and separation anxiety itself, speaks to the predominance of the father transference and the denial of the maternal transference – a source of much valuable therapeutic analysis. Men often want to relate to the therapist as if he is a mother but are unable to do so because they are afraid he will react like a father by shaming or humiliating him for his infantile needs for care and nurturing.

What I want to describe here is a more chronic form of this denial of attachment related states of mind. Donald Winnicott once said that 'the breakdown you fear is the breakdown that has already happened'.[2] I have always preferred to generalize this to 'the _____ you fear is the _____ that has already happened'. Fill in the blanks with the word of your choice. It has become a therapeutic cliché that men do not show depression and will go to great lengths to mask it. There are many reasons for this and I hope they will be clear by the end of this book. My own observation is that men suffer from powerful anxiety about loss in relationships – depressive anxiety – but are as resistant to acknowledging it as they are to acknowledging any vulnerability or dependency. The result is that this anxiety becomes free floating. Free floating anxiety is anxiety deriving from a broken connection between it and the precipitator. Detached attachment does not mean that the man only denies the connection between himself and the object of his attachment but also actively breaks mental connections between attachment related events and their consequences, e.g. breaks in treatment.

I have worked with many men who struggle chronically with fears of loss of a catastrophic nature. I think of the 40 year old man, a hypochondriac, who lived in constant fear of heart attack and myriad other illnesses although there was no history in his family and he had been so afraid since his early 20s (his heart had, of course, been broken when he was a child). Another lived in constant fear of losing all his money (his most valued internal object – whom he had already lost) although he had so much that he would have to do something extremely foolish or the world economic system would have to collapse for this to happen. I have written about him elsewhere in this book. Then there is the man who 'knew' he was going to be rejected by the woman he was currently involved with or the man who was equally convinced he was about to be dismissed from his job. I could multiply these examples a hundredfold. Of course they were not always unfounded anxieties. These anxieties can be so debilitating that men will often make them into self-fulfilling prophecies – they will behave in ways that bring about what they apparently fear most.

As I have said, I believe that masculinity is predicated on the separation from, and loss of, the maternal object as the little boy moves into the Oedipus complex – what I here call the 'fault' underpinning masculinity. As I shall explain, this loss and the consequent fault are denied and defended against with a masculinity based on phallic narcissism. I see this loss in clinical practice every day or at least I see the symptoms of its not having been fully metabolized but denied and repressed. One such manifestation of it is the presence of chronic anxieties about future loss. I believe that what men do is project the loss into the future in the hope that they can pre-empt or prevent it. What they do not realize is that they are already living with the loss and that the fear of the future loss is simply a distortion, but equally intense, of the loss they have already suffered. What I more generally see are the symptoms of anxiety denied – and this usually takes the form of acting out of some compulsive behaviour the origins of which they are at a loss to explain, e.g. seeing prostitutes, addiction to pornography, infidelity, drinking, gambling, perversion, etc. Naturally I am intensely interested in why the acting out takes the form is does. Unsurprisingly it is usually that behaviour which is the presenting complaint.

Separation anxiety and insecurity profoundly interfere with the capacity for establishing healthy close relationships with anybody. This is particularly so for men in relation to women. It is a commonplace observation that men are not good at intimacy. What this means is that men find it hard to be close to other people because it makes them anxious, but what does this mean in practice? The most obvious symptom of the anxiety is difficulty in being with someone for any length of time without engaging in some form of activity that removes the focus from the relationship or simply absents the man. We are usually quite good at being with people if it involves doing something together. I recall one young man, let us call him Daniel, who came to me because of a repeated pattern of getting deeply involved with a woman and then quickly developing panic attacks in her presence. Inevitably this led him to tell her that he was too ill to be with her. She would feel rejected and upset but invariably leave him as instructed. This would be followed by his getting suicidally depressed and very obsessed about her becoming involved with another man. His depression would then be potentiated by jealousy. Apart from these severe difficulties in relationships he found it very difficult to maintain any sort of career. His relationship with employers paralleled his relationships with women – an exciting start followed by serious doubts, anxiety and resignation from the job. He seemed incapable of maintaining any sort of life or career plan.

I am sure that all therapists are used to stories from patients about arguments or conflicts which occur late in the evening and inevitably lead to a frosty bedtime and no sexual intimacy. It is easy to see through the dynamics of such conflicts to the thinly disguised anxiety about intimacy which motivates the behaviour. In my experience such dynamics are reactive rather than systemic. They are a response to current difficulties which are unexpressed and unresolved and which make intimacy difficult rather than impossible. The difficulties experienced by Daniel were deeper and more profound than this. They went to the core of his personality and were omnipresent. It is relevant to say that he had been violently abused by his mother. He had never been hospitalized or seriously physically scarred, but the emotional and psychological damage were severe. When he responded by withdrawing from her or expressing his anger verbally she would apparently throw what he described as 'hysterical fits' and threaten to kill herself. This had gone on until he was well into his teens. Father was a passive, withdrawn inarticulate man whose sole interest outside work seemed to be horse racing and betting. After a few years he had developed his working life to the point where he was becoming quite successful but he had been through a number of relationships with women in which he had acted out the full drama described above. What struck me about his behaviour was that it was a more intense version of what many women complain about in men. They are charming and seductive and once they have you they withdraw and apparently lose interest for long periods without ever fully recovering the first full flush of passion and desire the women had experienced from him. This process can take a few years with most men but in Daniel's case it could be begun and finished in a week or even a weekend. His descent into depression was rapid and debilitating. His levels of distress were almost uncontainable and he would frequently drink or take drugs to escape the pain. It took very little time for him to realize that his predisposition to press a woman for a deep and intense commitment might be a major contributor to his difficulties. It was not uncommon for him to plan a holiday with someone he had known for only a few hours. Invariably, he was sexually intimate on the first date. He soon instituted a five date rule before becoming intimate but when he drank this rule would be easily over-ridden with all the familiar consequences. It is commonly said that one of the characteristics of men who abuse women is that they press for early intense commitment. I have worked with many abusive men and this is a common trait. However, I have worked with many men like Daniel who are not abusive and it is as common for them to press for early strong commitment. In fact, it seems to be a quality shared by the majority of men.[3]

There is a seeming paradox here. Why should a man press for such strong and early commitment if he is afraid of women? What is he afraid of? In Daniel's case he was afraid of being taken over. As soon as the woman made the commitment by responding to his practised charm offensive he would begin to feel trapped and claustrophobic. He wanted more than anything to be alone, to not be with her. This desire to reject, which he was unable to express, made him feel overwhelmingly guilty and depressed. Of course this was appropriate after all his efforts to entrap her. The obverse of this was his difficulty in being alone. Although he was often out of a relationship, he was rarely without a fantasy object, someone whom he was planning to be involved with. The capacity to be alone has been much explored. The inability to be alone is a limitation shared by the vast majority of men I have worked with as well as to abusive men.

As a result of my interest in masculinity and deviance I have had the opportunity to work in secure institutions that house mentally ill criminals. I was always much taken with Jim Gilligan's thesis about dangerous men in prisons.[4] His understanding was that many men act out violently in the prison system in order that they are never released because they are seen as so dangerous. His thinking is that they act out in order to ensure that they are never released in spite of all their protestations to the contrary that release is the thing they desire more than anything else. The point is that they are detained because they are so tough, so frightening, so masculine that society cannot cope with them. This is the reputation they earn within the system. The reality, according to Gilligan is that they are so needy and vulnerable and so incapable of caring for themselves that they are terrified of being released from the security of regular meals and a room and bed of their own. However, their masculine pride (phallic narcissism) is all they have left in a system of justice that has stripped them of all other routes to self-esteem. To frankly acknowledge their neediness and vulnerability would expose them to such shame and humiliation that it is unthinkable – hence the solution of being detained for being too much of a man!

I was unsure about this paradigm, although it could be seen as an orthodox psychodynamic explanation. It was only when I saw similar behaviour in institutions that I became convinced of its veracity. Many times I saw men, who were about to be released or discharged, act out in ways that were bound to prevent it. The frequency with which men on the brink of release (or male patients about to be discharged from mental hospital) would suffer a relapse or a regression into mad or bad behaviour was a convincing demonstration of unconscious processes in action. It is a testament to the power of phallic masculinity that men are prepared to be mad rather than frankly acknowledge their neediness and vulnerability in a setting where there is at least a chance of doing something positive about solving the problem other than becoming incompetent.

Hyper-masculine behaviours – those most designed to prove the power, strength and independence of the man – paradoxically mask the most powerful of overwhelming feelings of weakness, impotence, dependency and debilitating vulnerability. Hyper-masculine men are as disturbed as they are unhappy and suffering. Their need to take the big M to extremes speaks to the extremity of their anxiety and distress and the primitive nature of the trauma inflicted on them. Frightening others as a strategy for getting rid of one's own fear may provide temporary relief but it necessitates increasing and escalating doses to maintain a very fragile stability.

To sum up. One of the major therapeutic goals with men is to break down (or dissolve) their detachment. This is not possible without first deconstructing the fear of vulnerability and the denial of anxiety. The route to this is the analysis of normal forms of 'acting out' at times of obvious stress or threat.

3
The Fault – Its Origins and Nature

Ever since Freud wrote about it,[1] the Oedipus complex has been the subject of much heated discourse and discord. What the complex attempts is to provide an account of how little penis possessors become masculine and little non-penis possessors become feminine. Although it is clearly based on anatomical differences, they are not equivalent. The Oedipus complex is an attempt to account for gender division and this is not an anatomical distinction – sexual difference is anatomical – but a psychological and behavioural one which is taught and learned. I am always surprised that the idea of gender as being constructed rather than natural should cause any distress. It is a measure of Freud's radicalism that this is so. It is easily forgotten that the essential radicalism of early psychoanalysis was that it attempted to account for how identity becomes gendered.

I have already stated that I believe masculinity is not in crisis, but rather that masculinity is effectively a state of crisis, or a crisis management strategy, by virtue of its being effectively constructed on a structural fault. One way to imagine this is to think of a building erected on foundations which are not true vertical. One can go on building layers of brick on top of the foundations until the wall reaches true vertical but the structure will always be vulnerable to the possibility of total collapse back to the foundations if anything should move the walls.

Without conceding anything to the essentialists (who would have us believe that gender is natural – a given) I do believe that sexual division is pre-historical and that any historical differences can be explained and understood from within a constructionist paradigm.[2] The central tenet of what follows is that the trauma of the birth of the individual subject, the self, in the separation from the primary object, the mother, leads to what I have previously described (in *Men Who Batter Women*) as a gendered and encapsulated psychosis surrounded by primitive internalized sado-masochistic objects. Previously I have been interested to explain and account for men's violence and abusive behaviour to women as seen through that paradigm. In this work I have a different interest, although not one which completely ignores the role of violence and aggression in the male psyche but which places it amongst a basket of deviant behaviours used by men to prevent or avoid the fall into the fissure. Before I describe this fissure or fault which I believe underlies masculinity I need to take a brief detour.

It would be impossible to write a book about a dynamic approach to working with anybody without addressing the relationship between the notion of 'dynamic' and the idea of the unconscious. I will begin with a brief description of the unconscious.

The unconscious

Of course, everybody is nowadays familiar with the word unconscious and the fact that we are all supposed to have one. Its existence can be demonstrated with reference to what Freud called the 'psychopathology of everyday life'. In the book of the same name[3] he illustrated with examples such as forgetting that we can no longer take for granted that our conscious mind is in control of events within our minds or, indeed, our behaviour. He was not the first writer to make use of the term 'unconscious'. It had been used by many others long before he expanded and universalized it. At the start it was a shocking notion and not only because of the qualities with which Freud endowed it.

Even today, the construct cannot claim consensual status except within the psychoanalytic profession. There are respectable non-psychoanalytic therapists who have great difficulty with the idea of a structured, reified unconscious as Freud described it.

Freud's ideas are now well known. They have been widely disseminated and most people are familiar with the idea that our conscious self is not necessarily in control of our behaviour, feelings or thoughts. Nonetheless, there are still many unresolved logical and semantic difficulties with the idea even though it is generally accepted as a daily demonstrable fact of life that much of what we do, think and feel cannot be understood by reference to what is readily available in conscious functioning. It will be very hard for anyone to practise dynamic psychotherapy without some conceptual understanding of why this is so. Of course we are all familiar, and comfortable, with the idea of unconscious material. We all of us know that there is a great deal of knowledge and information which we know, and know that we know, and which can be called up when needed but which is not in consciousness. It is like a hard disk which we can access as necessary when we need the information it contains. This hard disk has the primary quality of unconsciousness; it is out of awareness. There is another sort of unconscious material, however, which is not accessible at will. This material is actually being kept unconscious. It is material which we do not want to know and do not know we know. Psychotherapists call this not wanting to know *resistance* and the process by which we hide material *defences*. For example, the fable of the fox who decided that the grapes were sour after he had tried, in vain, to reach them on the vine illustrates one way of rationalizing (the defence) failure – and keeping the pain at bay.

There are major differences in the way these two types of information are processed in the mind. The readily available hard drive obeys all the rules of formal thinking. It is logical, it is reality tested, it is linear in time and causality, it is not internally contradictory – we do not think that A which is opposite to B, is true when we also believe B to be true. These rules, which are essential for everyday living, are known as the rules of 'secondary process'. We all learn them with our acquisition of language and they are employed, for most of the time, by the conscious 'self'.

The second type of unconscious material – which we resist knowing and actively 'unknow' – obeys quite a different set of rules; the rules of 'primary process'. This part of the mind is almost a separate person inside all of us – a structurally separate part. It has a life of its own in which people and information are treated without regard for secondary process rules. Contradictions abound. Mutually exclusive truths coexist. Time is at a standstill, causality is not linear, information is not reality tested, internal reality rules. Something is true because we believe it to be true. Although there may be long periods when the conscious mind is the victor and has established hegemony, this victory is never finalized. It is a battle which has to be fought out over and over again. The healthier we are (from one point of view) the longer will consciousness be dominated by secondary process, but any of us can be overwhelmed at any time and primary processes can achieve dominance over our functioning – as in compulsions, depression or phobias or morbid feelings. These distinctions, and the existence of the two parts of the self are not always so clear in our minds. At one extreme is mental illness in which the conscious mind is overwhelmed by unconscious material. To an external observer this can be quite bewildering, particularly if one is talking to a floridly psychotic person in whom delusions and hallucinations alternate with moments of lucidity. Although in a less extreme way even most ordinary people will have experienced similar processes at times in their lives. In states of jealousy for example we are all capable of thinking the most appalling thoughts and having frightening impulses about someone we love. This temporary insanity seems bizarre when we later recover our equilibrium. Perhaps even more common are states of grief or mourning that can seem, to the sufferer, so similar to states of pathological depression. Normally optimistic and robust dispositions can be overcome by feelings of loss and despair bordering on the suicidal.

One of the most common signs of the imminent danger of a breach of the boundary between our unconscious and conscious selves is anxiety – we all experience anxiety. A simple example mentioned earlier and observable in every psychotherapeutic/ counselling practice, is the increasing anxiety felt by many patients as breaks in treatment loom closer. They will report the anxiety but are often completely unable to accept any interpretation which connects it to the upcoming break. The reasons for this are multiple and it is particularly observable in male patients in my experience. Usually it is not worthwhile making an interpretation until it has happened a few times and then only a gentle suggestion is called for. Plunging interpretations are usually resisted. In this case the threat is of loss and the anxiety is separation anxiety – probably the most debilitating and painful of all forms of anxiety. The loss is both the imminent one and, more importantly, the much older and unmetabolized experiences of loss the denial of which is essential for the patient to maintain his functioning.

Anxiety does not always imply the danger of an incursion of the unconscious into the conscious self – clearly there are many realistic sources of anxiety. These, however, can be employed by the unconscious and cause an excessively anxious response to quite ordinary sources of worry. This happens when an everyday event evokes in the unconscious mind echoes of situations which seem similar. All events are processed by the unconscious. The barrier works, in the main, in one direction only: from the unconscious to the conscious. The unconscious mind is primitive, infantile and dominated by passions. If it were to overwhelm the conscious self, normal functioning would be impossible. Anxiety is a signal that this might occur, and that the conscious self had better take avoiding action. Everything contains the potential for evoking primitive responses from us. Clearly, however, some of us are better defended than others against this possibility. What makes this so is an important question insofar as it is probably a major determinant of the extremity and intensity of a man's 'ordinary deviance' and the extent to which his behaviour is synchronous with his self-image.

There are simple everyday examples of the unconscious which most people experience and about which Freud wrote very amusingly in *The Psychopathology of Everyday Life*. Ordinary examples include forgetting, slips of the tongue, misreadings, mistakes or errors, etc. How many of us have not had the experience of saying something only to realize that we have used a word the direct opposite of the one we intended to use?

Compulsive or addictive behaviours are illustrative of unconscious conflict. Smoking when we know that it might kill us is one such behaviour. Most people will do something which they don't like or which causes them anxiety and yet they feel unable to stop it even though it conflicts with their value system or their morals or their self-image. They feel powerless in the face of the impulse. Such situations would not exist unless there is a part of the self which is not accessible to consciousness. Identity is not seamless. We all live with constant conflict.

In part this is because of another fundamental difference between the conscious and unconscious minds. Apart from the unconscious being dominated by primary (non-rational) processes, it is also essentially animalistic and is governed by the 'pleasure' principle whereas the conscious mind is governed by the 'reality' principle. The unconscious seeks nothing more than gratification of the impulse, whatever it may be. It is without conscience or values or morality. Under the influence of the pleasure principle, in which pain is avoided and satisfaction is sought, unconscious ideas, feelings, impulses and processes strive for expression in consciousness. 'Primary process' is basic. It is older than secondary process. It's objective is simple: gratification/satisfaction. Thinking, which is a secondary process, is inhibited action. It is not difficult to see why the conscious self should be in conflict with the unconscious when its only concern is gratification. The function of consciousness is to negotiate with reality and organize our lives to satisfy as much of our unconscious wishes as is possible and is commensurate with maintaining our membership of the community. Naturally, this does not apply to people who are suffering from mental illness and are overwhelmed with anxiety or with primary process. Obviously, secondary processes have survival value or would never have developed. Healthy individuals learn to be satisfied with achieving a compromise between the demands of reality and the demand for gratification. My patients fail in the task to differing degrees and develop symptoms. In general they come for psychotherapy because they want the symptoms removing. It is a common fantasy that there is a psychological equivalent to surgical removal. It is a source of disappointment when they learn that this is fallacious and that they cannot simply hand over the symptom as if it were an illness and I were a physician.

Anyone practising psychotherapy without placing the unconscious at the centre of her endeavours is not practising dynamic or analytic psychotherapy. For the reader to understand what follows she needs to accept its existence without question although its content is open to debate and disagreement. Let me now return to the fissure or fault underlying masculinity.

The Oedipus complex and misogyny

As I stated in the introduction, the words 'men' and 'masculinity' can cause a great deal of confusion. Most research into the differences between men and women conclude that, depending on what we measure, the differences between women are greater than the differences between men and women. However, there are two particular kinds of behaviour for which this is not the case: criminality (especially crimes of violence) and perversion. I said in the introduction that we should define masculinity empirically, that is by what men do rather than taking an 'essentialist' position and looking for some essential quality or qualities in men which are not possessed by women such as Freud did when he offered the opinion that women, unlike men, did not possess a superego or conscience. This reasoning puts me in rather an odd position. It might seem I am saying that what defines masculinity is the performance of criminal and or perverse behaviours, that all men are perverse or criminal. I want to make it clear that I am not saying this. What I am saying is that these forms of behaviour are predominantly acted out by men and that if we want to understand men we need to understand what it is about men that they act in these ways whilst women, in general, do not. It may be that by pursuing this line of enquiry we will reach an understanding of men which illustrates some 'essential' difference in the way that little boys are raised that produces these behavioural differences and which do not apply to little girls. Although this is not a study in child rearing practices, I think it is important to understand how boys and girls are differentially treated during childhood and how this contributes to what men think being a man entails.

For the moment I want to set the intellectual frame for the book by taking a close look at the paradigm that set the tone for all the major debates about gender formation and gender identity after the 19th century – the Freudian, psychoanalytic, paradigm. Freud set out his most important thinking about gender formation in a series of writings beginning with a hint in a letter to Fleiss in 1886.[4] From then on it developed richness and complexity with every appearance and he was still absorbed by it in his *Outline of Psychoanalysis* published in 1940.[5] It was not for nothing that he was so absorbed by the Oedipus myth. His writings about it are the cornerstone of the content of analysis if not of the meta-psychology. It introduced into the world of paediatrics the idea of a child full of passionate feelings of love and hate towards his parents. If we owe him nothing else we owe to Freud the legacy of seeing children as actors in the family drama who are not merely *tabula rasa* (clean slates) onto which the family or society can write what they wish. He introduced to us a child with an internal world of incredible richness, savagery, lust and jealous passion. It is to my mind unfortunate that the language of the Oedipus complex has entered everyday language insofar as it creates the illusion that by knowing the myth we understand Freud's unique re-writing of it. It would be misleading to pretend that it is not without its detractors and deniers but I am convinced that it is impossible to understand the psychological development of masculinity without an understanding of the complex.

It was perhaps the most shocking finding of Freud's research, into infantile development as revealed and reconstructed in his consulting room, that from about the age of three the child begins to experience his love for his mother in a rather more specifically sexual way than previously. In fact he wants to marry her and be the father of her children! This is the so called positive Oedipus complex. Many parents will also know the parallel is that little girls want to marry daddy when they grow up. In the simplest possible terms this brings the boy into direct rivalry with his father. Clearly this is an untenable position for the little boy. Life would be unbearable for him if he could not find a solution to his conflict. Rivalry or competition is fundamentally the wish to kill one's competitors. Part of the significance of the Oedipus complex is that it took psychoanalysis into the social world of three-body relationships and out of the undifferentiated two-body relationship between the child and mother. Let me also say at this point that although much is made in Freudian theory of penis envy in females, my experience gained from working with hundreds of men is that penis envy is more a problem for them than it is for women. It is men who go to watch phallic action heroes in the many Hollywood blockbusters in this genre. Bruce Willis, Arnold Schwarzenegger, Steven Seagal and others are the object of envy for men because they embody, or are portrayed as embodying, all the qualities for which phallic masculinity is admired. They are unafraid. They need nobody. They can defeat any man in armed or unarmed combat. Women are portrayed as being in awe of them and flattered to be desired by them. They do not suffer anxiety or depression or any other form of vulnerability. They are MUSCULAR! They have muscles everywhere. Their whole body is one giant erect penis capable of bursting through any obstacle. I could go on (and on), but will spare the reader any more embarrassment. It needs little analytic skill to see that this is more than likely the way a little boy sees his father, and the way a father might present himself to his little boy, albeit unintentionally. Also, the roots of penis envy in men will be found in their perceptions of their all-powerful fathers during the resolution, or not, of the Oedipus complex.

This combination of homicidal competitiveness and envy versus love and admiration causes intense anxiety in the little boy and an urgent need to find a solution. In order to understand how this comes about it is important to understand what Freud called 'universal phallic monism'. This is the assumption made by the boy that everyone in the world has a penis. As we shall see, this is a rather crucial piece of Freudian theory insofar as Freudian psychoanalysis is erected (so to speak) on it. It is the discovery or the realization (discovering what he already knew) that his mother does not possess one that provides the motive force for resolving or dissolving the complex. This discovery terrifies the child because he imagines that this is what will become of him – his father will cut off his penis (so called castration anxiety) – if he does not relinquish his desire for his mother.

The crucial factor here is the boy's wholly mistaken deduction that his mother lacks a penis because his father castrated her during their love making. Freud believed that children would overhear and perhaps even see the parents and misinterpret the sounds as indicating the father making a violent attack on the mother; he called this the fantasy of the primal scene. Love making is seen as a sado-masochistic act essentially; an act of dominance involving rape and physical damage. Of course this fantasy of violence is fed by the boy's projection of his own violent feelings towards the couple deriving from his feelings of rejection, betrayal and jealousy. Actual sight or sound of the united couple is not, however, necessary for primal scene fantasy to occur. He may have no knowledge of it at all, but he will be aware that something is going on between his parents, from which he is excluded and that arouses his interest and excitement and the same jealous passions. Incidentally, this is one of the two root causes or sources of all feelings of exclusion – the other being the exclusion from the parent/sibling bond. The common insecurity articulated by patients that 'no-one ever calls, everyone is at a party and I'm the only one not invited' has its root here – outside the parental bedroom door! Alongside this is an acute anxiety of what his father might do to him if he were to be aware of the child's homicidal feelings towards him and his desire to take his place with the mother. This anxiety, castration anxiety as it is known, is what propels the boy into the phase of resolution of his positive Oedipus complex.

In the broadest terms, as a result of his fear of castration if he does not relinquish his mother, the boy begins the process of identifying with his father and dis-identifying with his mother.[6] As we shall see, this is an elegant solution. During this process he sees, increasingly, his mother as incomplete, as castrated. This precipitates a construction of her as worthy of contempt because she lacks a penis which, by this time, has become an object of veneration. In fact it has become more than a penis; it has become, symbolically, a phallus, a representation of the power of the father over the mother and the power of men in the world to which he aspires.

Schematically, this account of the boy's sexual development has a great deal to recommend it. Functionally, the boy's contempt for the castrated woman paves the way for his final development as a male by enabling him to identify with is father. This allows his fragile 'gender identity' to become more firmly established. Gender identity is the individual's sense of themselves as belonging to a particular sex. One question which is important to me, and this book, is why it is that the child should choose, from all the potential reactions, to feel contempt (what Freud called 'normal contempt') for his mother rather than sorrow or concern because she lacks a penis. I believe this has two sources and, as I understand them, they both contribute to the fault underlying masculinity.

Firstly, it seems to me that this contempt has it roots in the boy's earlier relations with his mother. Prior to the Oedipus complex the boy lives with the experience of his mother's omnipotence – she literally has the power of life and death over him. This is no idle fear and it persists in the unconscious mind of adult men to a potentially debilitating degree. I believe that the boy's contempt for his 'castrated' mother, whatever its functional value for his masculine development, rests on a reversal of his earlier feelings of impotence in relation to her. In ordinary circumstances (where the parents have no unusual pathology and are not poor or deprived) this impotence is not experienced by the child as disturbing until he is frustrated in his desire for the mother or primary attachment object. In fact I think we can assume that there is a period for most people when the attachment to the mother is almost blissful or 'oceanic'. The urge to merge with the breast/body of the mother is strong and is based on the desire to not be separated from the source of such pleasure and security. Adult experiences of sexual union are derived no doubt from these early primitive precursors.

As Melanie Klein pointed out,[7] contempt is a defence against envy – sour grapes being the commonest representation of this. So the boy's contempt for his mother and, later, women in general, is also a solution to his deep envy of her and her body and its contents which he wants entirely for himself and cannot have. Her possession of all he needed for survival and growth was the origin of his deep attachment to her and then became a source of envy when he realized she was beyond his control and, more importantly, controlled his access to her body. In spite of this I believe that men never relinquish the desire for total possession and control of his primary object and the later inheritor of the transference, his adult partner. Unfortunately, that envy, which has its origins in love and admiration, is a very destructive force. Envy wants to destroy the envied object. This is highly problematic for the male child because he also still desires her and wants to preserve her. The struggles to reconcile these opposing impulses led Klein to posit the existence of the paranoid/schizoid and depressive positions in which she described how the child goes about this overwhelmingly difficult task – a task which is never complete and a conflict which lives with most men for the rest of our lives. Few of us relinquish the desire to both merge with the object of desire (m/other) and simultaneously destroy her. As we shall see, I believe men achieve this by simultaneously idealizing women as sexual objects and denigrating them by denying them subjectivity.

Secondly, after the Oedipus complex, the boy's mother is now impotent because she lacks the all-powerful phallus – she is castrated. Whereas she once possessed all the good things of life and frustrated him by denying them, he now reverses the situation by seeing himself, a male, as having the good thing – the penis – and her, a female, as being deprived. He will also be dimly aware by this time that having a penis is correlated with real dominance and control in the world at large (more strictly speaking, the Phallus. The penis is a rather insignificant piece of flesh, although it supports a mighty weight!)

The move from envious dependency and the depressive position into the Oedipus complex requires that the child renounces the mother and dis-identifies from her in order to clear the way for the identification with the father which forms the basis of his move out of the Oedipus complex and into the gendered social world. This renunciation and dis-identification is the origin of the fault. On one side lies femininity, dependency, passivity, vulnerability and emotionality. On the other side, the side of the penis, lies masculinity, potency, activity, independence and strength; in other words, Phallic Narcissism.

In my view, this process is what leaves men, as a gender, with the capacity to both idealize and denigrate women and for these opposed internal images to be unreconciled and split from each other.

Robert Stoller describes how this reversal from impotence to omnipotence, disaster to triumph and masochism to sadism (passive to active) influences sexual fantasy and perversion.[8] He expresses the opinion that no man ever has sexual intercourse, even with someone he loves, without hostility. However, I do not think Stoller is sufficiently aware of the extent to which normal heterosexual relations are characterized by sadism inflicted by men on women they love (see my *Men Who Batter Women*).

Phallic narcissism and castration anxiety

In my view, although Freud can be credited with the discovery of phallic narcissism I believe he failed to appreciate how powerful a force it is and how wide ranging is its importance in the shaping of masculinity and men. In my opinion, Jacques Lacan completed this with his re-reading of Freud and his insights into the role of the phallus. There are hardly any male activities of any importance which are not, at unconscious root, designed to demonstrate the size and potency of the penis or, as Lacan[9] would have it given that it functions in the symbolic register, the phallus. Jean Laplanche and Jean-Bertrand Pontalis have this to say about Freud's account of the phallic phase:

> from the genetic point of view, the 'pair of opposites' constituted by activity and passivity, which is dominant during the anal stage, is transformed into the polarity of phallic and castrated; only at puberty is the opposition between masculinity and femininity established.
>
> So far as the Oedipus complex is concerned, the existence of a phallic stage has an essential role; the dissolution of the complex (in the case of the boy) is determined by the threat of castration, *the effectiveness of which depends first on the narcissistic interest directed by the little boy towards his own penis* [my emphasis] and secondly on his discovery of the lack of a penis in the little girl.[10]

Freud's main papers on the phallic phase clearly indicate the importance he attached to it in the development of masculinity. Without it, there could be no masculinity as we understand it in the psycho-analytic paradigm. What I think Freud understood but failed to stress, is the extent to which all 'male' activities (as socially and culturally understood) are infused with phallic narcissism – in other words with the possession of a penis and everything that it stands for. Conversely, all non-male activities come to represent what it is that phallic narcissism has come to mean – castration. What this reduces to is the understanding that everything a man believes to be male will potentiate his masculine self-esteem and everything he believes to be female (and by this I mean both activities *and* experiences) will evoke in him the anxiety which pushed him into the Oedipus complex in the first place, i.e. castration anxiety. On the other side of castration anxiety lies the fault constituted by the 'decision' to dis-identify from the mother and relinquish her as an object of desire. On the other side of the fault lies femininity, impotence, helplessness, dependency and passivity. This hypothesis explains much which otherwise remains obscure and which it is the goal of this book to explain.

Now we come to the core of my central hypothesis about masculinity and men. The phallus – by which I mean not the penis but everything it has come to symbolize, actions and feelings associated with being a man and masculine – unconsciously is a symbol of what it is intended to deny. To put it baldly, that is the central knowledge that *we are already and have always been castrated*. In fact, castration is the underlying experience of being male. More exactly, the underlying experience is of being penis-less insofar as the valuation attached to the penis is a development of the phallic phase which lies on the masculine side of the fault. We need to understand how the underlying castration is structured and its effects on the development of masculinity if we are to approach even a minimal understanding of adult male behaviour. The already existing castration has two sources. The first is the already described vulnerability and neediness in relation to the all-powerful mother or primary object and the underlying anxiety about her omnipotence in relation to the child – this is no fantasy. Without 'her' he could not exist – she really has the power of life and death. Simple separation from her is sufficient to cause annihilation anxiety and fears of psychological dissolution. This can be seen only too readily in some men when they lose their adult partner and realize, belatedly, that she is the scaffolding which has held together his fragile psyche. The second source is the realization that the object of his desire and his passion already belongs to someone infinitely more powerful than himself – his father in relation to whom he is small and helpless. So on both counts the little boy's entrance into the social world is characterized by failure, fear and impotence. The promise of an identification with his father is that he will possess what he envies so much about his father – his power, strength, invulnerability and, eventually in effigy, the maternal object. However, it will also require him to metabolize his fiercely competitive feelings and he will do this eventually by generalizing them to his relations with all men. Make no mistake however; they are little different from his competitive feelings towards his own father and contain the same desires to destroy physically or psychologically by shaming or humiliating other men. The desire to defeat other men and humiliate and shame them is an attempt to project the original feelings of shame and humiliation he felt when he realized that he could never defeat his father and that his father would always be more powerful than he could be insofar as the child could never possess the ultimate object of his desire, his mother. So masculinity is predicated on the experience of loss and failure, shame and humiliation, and the fear of more of the same if the little boy does not identify with his father and resolve his castration anxiety. Much of his life the boy-become-man will occupy himself with activities, or fantasy which has at its centre the search for status and power. This drive for power and status is fundamentally a defence against the underlying truth, the already existing castration with all that this implies and against which so many men struggle to defend or attempt to deny. Much, if not most masculine activity is motivated by wounded phallic narcissism; by the shame, humiliation and vulnerabililty of failure, impotence, fear and weakness masquerading as its opposite – the big M as I have called it. I need to point out, if it is not already clear, that the Oedipal father is also a fantasy. He possesses those powers in relation only to children and subjugated women. However, this does not prevent men from trying to achieve this phallic omnipotence throughout their adult lives until inevitable decay arrives.

So, the fear of castration or of losing his penis, at that time his most prized possession, is the fundamental element in the little boy's decision to relinquish his mother as an object of desire and ownership and this depends primarily on the valuation he places on his penis. As I have already pointed out, by this time the little boy has discovered the pleasure to be gained from playing with his penis and the comfort to be derived from doing so. Initially, the experience of erections can be discomforting to the boy. I remember my grandson describing how there was 'a bone in his willy' when he was three years old and that it was not nice. This quickly developed into 'too many bones in my willy!' prior to the cessation of the complaints about the experience!

My conclusion from this is that although we speak of the 'resolution of the Oedipus complex', and the routes to it, I do not believe any of the men I have worked with would meet the description of having resolved the complex. Unless, that is, we were to describe its resolution as a state in which the tension and conflict between the masculine and feminine elements in the personality is thoughtfully held and contained. The key word here is 'contained' by which I mean held in the mind in a thoughtful way and in which thought is a substitute for action or acting out of the polar extremes. This is a process that is not complete until young manhood and definitely post teens.

Schematically this relinquishment describes the positive Oedipus complex in which the mother is the loved object and the father is the rival. It is positive insofar as it represents society's desired outcome of heterosexual object choice. However, there is also a negative Oedipus complex in which the father is the desired object and the mother is the rival. According to traditional Freudian theory, the resolution of the full Oedipus complex – the negative and the positive – determines the individual's gender identity and object choice.

The negative Oedipus complex[11]

Much of this book is taken up with descriptions of male sexual behaviour which do not fit stereotypical or normative representations of masculinity. To my mind, the normal deviations described in these case studies are the result of an incomplete resolution of the full Oedipus complex and particularly the Negative version. I would go further in saying that these deviations are symptomatic of the impossibility of Oedipal resolution. In the Oedipal model Freud set up a psycho-social conundrum which, although not intended to, implicitly functioned to resolve a whole series of only apparently contradictory biological processes the open expression of which is threatening to social order.[12]

The negative Oedipus complex is the homosexual element of the child's innate bisexuality which leads him or her to desire the parent of the same sex and see the opposite sex parent as the rival. Of course, as Freud pointed out, the intensity of the homosexual part of the constitution will vary from person to person – in some it will be the stronger and in others hardly noticeable. (I accept that with this acknowledgement, Freud could be accused of wanting it all ways. Where psychoanalytic theory could not explain he could fall back on a biology which was not deterministic but merely accounted for individual variation on a universal – and essential, indeed crucial – psychoanalytic theme.) The boy's homosexuality will generate in him passive fantasies of being penetrated by his father's penis or of otherwise incorporating it, for example orally. According to Freud, these fantasies will precipitate terrifying anxieties about the possibility of losing his penis in the light of his re-interpretation of the knowledge that his mother does not possess one and most likely lost it during sexual activity with the father. The boy 'relinquishes' his incestuous desire for his mother by identifying with his father under the influence of castration anxiety. By identifying with the father his mother becomes the unconscious object of desire through that identification. Simultaneously he deals with his castration anxiety by relinquishing his father as the object of desire – a desire which could be problematic should he identify with the mother. However, the fate of his negative complex is determined by the strength of his homosexual inclination – a return to the biological in Freudian thinking and, in my view, entirely unnecessary. The assumption of a constitution implies an acceptance of something 'essential' about human sexuality by which I mean innate or biologically determined. I do not subscribe to such a position. As we shall see, I hold to a position that human sexuality is entirely socially constructed and that it is no more natural for a man to want to penetrate a vagina than to penetrate a can of liver, an orange or a hole in a tree. By the same token I do not believe there is a 'natural' desire in women to be penetrated, nor to be penetrated by an erect penis. Like Gore Vidal, I do not believe in homosexuality or heterosexuality. There are homo and heterosexual acts. However, from a psychoanalytic viewpoint, I have to take being 'gay' seriously. When a patient presents with problems related to a construction of himself with a 'gay' identity I have no choice. Nonetheless, I also see this as being a relatively recent invention along with the invention of many new identities in our 'post-modernist' world. I understand this proliferation of identities as a reflection of a 'crisis of identity' related to the evolution of trans-global capitalism and the politics of global economic processes with all the concurrent fragmentation of social and cultural institutions that this evolution has necessitated.

One of the consequences of the negative Oedipus complex is that men can be left with a deeply ambivalent and confused relationship with the penis, their own and others. It is at one and the same time an object of veneration as the source of great pleasure, and fear as the source of so much anxiety connected with the fear of losing it – one's own – and the desire to incorporate it – the other's – with all the attendant homosexual anxiety, even panic, that that can evoke. Much of adult male sexual ordinary deviance can be understood as a product of these conflicts. We inevitably have deep homosexual conflicts when we love our own penis so much and have to resolve all manner of difficulties in relationships with other men and their penises (the existence of which is normally denied by heterosexual men). During puberty, the passive homosexual desires undergo repression and sublimation into male friendship and bonding activities which are often only thinly disguised.

If I do not follow Freud's adherence to the biological in his understanding of homosexuality, then what paradigm can I use to unpack the problems of male sexuality? It is implicit in what I have said above about the social construction of sexuality. Sexual behaviour is just that – it is not straight or gay or bisexual. We do not label other animal sexual behaviour in the same way. Our need to label sexuality and sexual behaviour has deep psycho-political significance and it is more derived from the need to control sexual behaviour because of unconscious fears of the social consequences of uncontrolled sexuality. I hold to the view that all sexuality is intrinsically polymorphous (not polymor-phously perverse as Freud described it) and that it is indifferent with respect to aim and object until it is shaped by social and cultural influences as presented by the parents or primary carers and then the wider social world.

As we can see from the case studies here, the difficulty in metabolizing the identification with the mother in her sexual relations with the father – as being penetrated by and containing the penis – at the same time as the identification with the father as penetrating and having the penis can explain many of what I refer to as 'ordinary deviations' in men. Later case studies will illustrate the vicissitudes of this conflict and the opposing iden-tifications in the context of the constant search for the breast.

4
Attachment and Masculinity

Although I have already discussed intimacy and attachment as a special case in men's treatment, some aspects of attachment theory are worthy of deeper consideration considering that men's attachment style is, alongside the penis, one of the foundation stones of masculinity.[1]

If we asked most women I suspect they will tell us that men have great difficulty in acknowledging that their female partner means a lot to them, or that the attachment is of any real significance. Suspicion aside, I can be sure that the vast majority of men I have worked with found it very difficult to acknowledge until they were threatened with the loss of the attachment. Furthermore, this is generalized to denying that any attachment is particularly significant. Of course there are variations in the degree but the capacity for such attachment denial has been a noticeable quality in my male patients. Attachment research tells us that with similar troubled attachment histories in childhood, little boys grow into men who have externalizing pathology and little girls grow into women who have internalizing pathology. To put it simply, men act out and women become anxious and depressed. Another way of putting it would be to say that when the going gets tough women becoming disturbed and men become disturbing; men punish others whilst women punish themselves. Again we get to the connection between activity and masculinity and femininity and passivity.

One notices this in the transference. After the initial phase when one begins to notice the standard reactions to breaks in treatment (although this clearly takes longer if one is seeing someone only once a week) interpretations relating this to feelings of abandonment or separation anxiety for example, are often met with incredulous laughter and comments about my narcissism and grandiosity. The idea that they might have formed an attachment to me and that its loss or interruption could be the cause of distress is risible for the vast majority of the men I have worked with, at least at the outset. This is not simply related to the relationship with me as therapist, it infiltrates every aspect of these men's lives. It is as if the idea of their being attached, which they conflate with the idea of being dependent in a relationship, is unthinkable and for it to be with a man is even more unthinkable as it arouses homosexual anxieties. I remember in the film *Analyze This* when the gangster first met the analyst he said, 'Make me a fag and you're dead!' Unsurprisingly he ended by being very dependent on the analyst. In fact, more often than not men complain about being in a relationship with a woman who is dependent on them and the man finds this intolerable. Of course their intolerance of this derives from the woman getting away with something he unconsciously yearns for and consciously derides and denigrates. In spite of this, men continue to seek attachment or at least imitations of it throughout their lives. Indeed, many stay in exclusive relationships for the whole of their lives (even though few of them, if we believe the surveys, are monogamous or faithful). How can it be that a need which is so central to life (if we are to believe John Bowlby, the discoverer of attachment processes) can be denied at the same time as it is so actively pursued? There is no doubt that men appreciate the value of attachment in practice even if they consciously or manifestly minimize or deny outright its importance. The research is clear and it is supported by our daily observations and personal experience. People prefer to be in relationships rather than alone. It is probably the most fundamental motivation for human behaviour (underpinned no doubt by a selfish gene) and, as one vastly experienced attachment therapist from the

Tavistock Clinic has said, 'is responsible for the anxiety which drives 95% of human behaviour!'

What can we say about men and attachment that will illuminate the perverse behaviour described above? Bowlby's seminal work, *Attachment and Loss*,[2] described in detail the fundamental importance to human beings of attachment and he described the basic styles of attachment and their origins in early patterns of relationships with primary carers. An attachment style can be defined as a strategy for regulating feelings of security in close relationships. The style refers to repetitive patterns of behaviour in relation to the attachment object which are aimed at evoking and ensuring predictable responses from the object. Although it is clear from his writings that attachment is value neutral, i.e. no one form of attachment is better than any other, his work has been colonized, quite rightly some would say, by the mental health industry such that of all the available forms of attachment style it is the secure style which has come to be the touchstone of mental and social health and to which we should all aspire. Most people use a four category model of adult attachment.[3] These four styles are:

1. Secure
2. Fearful
3. Preoccupied
4. Dismissing

Before describing briefly the distinguishing qualities and aetiology of each of these styles I want to add a caveat.

It needs to be said that the concept of an attachment style requires a marriage to another concept in order for it to make sense. That second concept is of an 'Internal Working Model'. An IWM is a mental model of the self in relation to others. As described below by Horowitz, Rosenberg and Bartholomew,

Bowlby put forward the fairly orthodox psychoanalytic notion (at least in psychoanalytic object relations theory) that,

> over time children internalize early attachment experiences and use these internal representations (models) to judge whether or not the attachment figure is the sort of person who responds to calls for support and protection and whether or not the self is the sort of person towards whom anyone, and the attachment figure in particular, is likely to respond in a helpful way. The first judgement concerns the child's image of other people and the second concerns the child's image of the self.[4]

Horowitz, Rosenberg and Bartholomew do something very interesting with the notion of internal working models of self and other. They conceptualize the models as continua of worthiness such that there can be a positive and negative image of self and a positive or negative image of the other. This provides four attachment patterns or styles (see Figure 4.1).

> Each cell [in Figure 4.1] represents a theoretical ideal of an attachment style. Cell 1 indicates a sense of worthiness (lovability) plus an expectation that other people are generally accepting and responsive. This cell corresponds to a category that other investigators have called securely attached. We call it secure. Cell 2 indicates a sense of unworthiness (unlovability) combined with a positive evaluation of others, leading the person to strive for self-acceptance by gaining the acceptance of valued others. It corresponds to Hazan and Shaver's ambivalent group and to Main's enmeshed or preoccupied with attachment pattern; we call it preoccupied. Cell 3 indicates a sense of unworthiness combined with an expectation that others will be negatively disposed (untrustworthy, rejecting). By avoiding close involvement with others, people using this style are able to protect themselves against anticipated rejection... it corresponds in part to the avoidant style described by Hazan and Shaver (1987) – we call it fearful/avoidant. Finally, cell 4 indicates a sense of worthiness combined with a negative disposition toward other people. Such people protect themselves against disappointment by avoiding close relationships and maintaining a sense of independence and invulnerability. This style corresponds conceptually to the detached or

dismissing-of-attachment attitude described by Main et al (1985); we call it dismissive/avoidant.[5]

	Model of Self	
	Positive	Negative
Positive	CELL I SECURE Comfortable with intimacy and autonomy	CELL II PREOCCUPIED Preoccupied with relationships
Negative	CELL IV DISMISSING Dismissing of intimacy Counter-dependent	CELL III FEARFUL Fearful of intimacy Socially avoidant

Model of Other

Figure 4.1 Four theoretical attachment styles

Source: L.M. Horowitz, S.E. Rosenberg and K. Bartholomew. 'Interpersonal problems, attachment styles, and outcome in brief psychotherapy'. 1993. *J. Cons. and Cl. Psy.* 61:549–560.

As Griffin and Bartholomew describe this conceptualization or systematization of IWM: 'the positivity of the self model indicates the degree of anxiety and dependency experienced in close relationships; the other model is associated with the tendency to seek out or avoid closeness in relationships'.[6] Those older readers with a history of catholic tastes in psychotherapy theory will be strongly reminded of Thomas Harris' *I'm OK, You're OK*,[7] a much beloved text for transactional analysts which describes these self and other models in some detail.

From a mental health point of view the secure style is the desirable attachment style although it is important to say that no one style is better than any other – it depends entirely on environmental fit and adaptation. Although there are probably many counsellors who have seen patients who are predominantly secure and undergoing some sort of temporary or acute life crisis, I have never seen anyone in my long career who could be diagnosed as being possessed of a dominant secure attachment style. In fact a great many people seek psychotherapy precisely because they are unable to feel secure in a relationship and are lacking a positive internal object. It speaks volumes for the success of psychotherapy and the mental health industry in disseminating their values that people feel inadequate if they are unable to live up to them. Apart from the conspicuous absence of securely attached people in long term treatment (at least with me) is the concordance between different styles of attachment and gender. I realize that many therapists will not agree with me, but I have observed from the many men I have treated that they are generally dismissive of attachments and the more so when they feel dependent. In a minority of cases they are preoccupied or avoidant but without doubt dismissiveness has been the dominant and characteristic attachment style of the men in my practice. For those who know my work it will come as no surprise when I say that the largest single group of men in my practice (approx 40%) has been men who are violent or sexually perverse or who suffer from addictions (often in combination). I freely acknowledge that a life spent with so many apparently extreme types could lead one to both a jaundiced and distorted perception of men and masculinity and that it therefore might be difficult to make any defensible statements about non-patient men in general from such experience. Nonetheless I am prepared to take the risk of such a charge.

In my work I am often reminded of Freud's remark that there were very few occasions when he was unable to identify with anything told him by his patients. This is certainly true of my work with men. It rarely happens that they tell me anything that is so alien that I cannot find at least an echo of it in myself no matter how extreme or perverse. This has led me to the firm belief that what unites us as men is more significant than what divides us and that such divisions are more quantitative than qualitative. However, let's look at the links between masculinity and attachment.

My friend and colleague Gwen Adshead (an exceptional consultant psychotherapist at Broadmoor Hospital which houses some of the most dangerous criminals in the UK) once gave me a simple description of a pervert. It is a man who simultaneously idealizes and is contemptuous of women – he unconsciously hates them; he is either dismissive of attachment or avoidant, incapable of intimacy and relates to sexualized part objects or object substitutes. I remember saying, half jokingly, that this sounded like a description of most men I know and that she was unwittingly defining masculinity as a perversion. She laughed as she informed me that it was not unwitting and that it was not entirely a joke; that although it was extreme, some radical feminists (which she is not) make a case for a definition of masculinity indistinguishable from a definition of perversity. One other remarkable thing about perversity of course is that it is almost entirely a male preserve.

I am sure that you can spot the first link between attachment and the histories I presented earlier – that between dismissiveness or avoidance and perversity. The link between dismissiveness and perversity is well established clinically

Let's take a closer look at attachment styles and their implications for relationships and the structure of the internal world.

SECURE: Positive self-model, positive other-model

Key features: high coherence, high self-confidence without grandiosity or narcissism, positive approach to others, high intimacy in relationships.

Secure individuals are fluent and thoughtful. They have learned from their past relationship experiences, and are able to evaluate current and past relationships realistically. They come across as warm and likeable and as generally positive about life and realistically optimistic about the future.

Secure individuals are flexible in responding to difficulty in personal matters. They do not respond passively to problems, by denying them or withdrawing from them, but instead they address the difficulty and use a variety of strategies. They are able to turn to others for support and help when required and they will not feel shame about it or that they have failed.

Secure individuals have good self-esteem which is not grandiose or unrealistic. They have a clear sense of their limitations and find security in this knowledge. They are self-confident and trust their reactions to people and events but are able to check reality if necessary. They do not suffer from stranger anxiety or inappropriate performance anxiety and are able to let others know when they feel badly treated. They have no difficulty with emotional dependency which is usually of only moderate intensity. They commonly spread their dependencies and don't expect any one relationship to be able to provide for all their emotional needs. They will not sacrifice their friendships for a romantic attachment and can respond to loss with appropriate grief without total collapse or breakdown.

Secure individuals see others in a positive way. They like other people and are capable of demonstrating warmth and affection. They seek out other people and are comfortable expressing a range of emotions to others when appropriate. They try to solve conflict constructively and they are comfortable living with difference in their relationships and can find it a source of richness rather than a threat. Secure people tend to be seen as reliable, friendly and warm. This sounds rather idealized and reminds me of the Victorian analytic descriptions of the fully resolved Oedipal character. It needs to be said that secure individuals are not all temperamentally the same. They can be quiet or extroverted but they are basically sociable and like and appreciate others.

Although their romantic attachments show many of the qualities mentioned above – intimacy, closeness, mutual respect and involvement, disclosure, etc. – this does not mean they have perfect relationships, even if we knew what that might be like, but they are realistic in their appraisals of their partners and the difficulties in their relationships. If they are not in a romantic attachment they do not rush into one out of anxiety or loneliness. They can tolerate loneliness without despair.

FEARFUL: Negative self-model, negative other-model

Key features: lack self-confidence. They both want and fear close relationships. They are afraid of rejection and cope by avoiding closeness with others. They can be self-conscious to the point where some of their thinking about being observed can seem paranoid.

Fearful individuals come across as anxious, insecure, vulnerable and self-conscious. They laugh nervously when they are not amused. They suffer from stranger anxiety but can start to feel safe after a while and allow themselves to feel intimate. When this happens they may become very disclosing as if they are relieved to finally have found a non-judgemental person to listen to them.

When there are difficulties in their life fearful people are emotionally reactive and do not actively deal with their distress. Rather they will feel overwhelmed and at a loss about what to do to solve the problems. They don't ask for help or support. They are not in denial; they know they feel bad but they are afraid to display their distress in front of others. They are not emotionally expressive, and don't cry in front of others until they feel very safe.

Fearful individuals have negative self-models. They have low self-confidence and are very self-critical. They are highly emotionally dependent, very jealous, and suffer from high levels of separation anxiety. They are likely to think that others don't like them, or that others view them as stupid, unattractive, or boring. Fearful individuals will typically say that they wish to open up more or to become more socially confident.

Fearful individuals have difficulty developing trust. They want contact with others but they feel that they don't 'fit in' and are extremely sensitive to any signs of rejection. When they are in relationships, they are dependent, and they feel lonely. They are also likely to worry about never finding a partner. In relationships, no matter how secure it might seem from outside, they will need frequent re-assurance that they will not be left or abandoned. However, as Freud said, you can't re-assure a neurotic. No matter how much they receive they will not believe it. Their default position is that nobody could possibly want them.

Fearful people have a negative internal working model of others. They will not ask for support unless they feel certain of not being rejected. They avoid conflict, or the open expression of feelings, because they are afraid of rejection. They are uncomfortable with affection, especially in public. They are shy and self-conscious.

Fearful individuals are likely to have taken years to establish the few close friendships they have. They feel more invested in their relationships than their friends and are less in control of the course of the friendships.

Fearful individuals find it difficult to become romantically involved for fear of being rejected or seen in a negative light. When involved in a romantic relationship they are very passive/dependent, and tend to be more invested than their partner. They have a hard time breaking off relationships because of their fear of ever finding another.

PREOCCUPIED: Negative self-model, positive other-model

Key features: preoccupied with relationships, idealizing but confused in discussing relationships, highly dependent on others for self-esteem.

Preoccupied individuals are highly emotionally expressive and, although fluent, can seem incoherent. They shift between idealizing and devaluing significant others, frequently contradict themselves, and, in general, show a lack of clarity and objectivity in discussing their close relationships.

They are emotionally reactive and can seem histrionic. In difficulty preoccupied individuals react very strongly or overreact. They have difficulty in dealing with their problems without help; their impulse is to immediately go to others when they feel bad. They are overly sensitive and cry frequently. They are uncontained and lack the capacity for affect regulation.

They have a negative self-model, little confidence and tend to be highly dependent on others for self-esteem. Alongside this they have a positive other-model. They are desperate for the company and attention of others, and tend to be overly demanding of closeness in relationships. They are too affectionate and have an insatiable need for attention and approval that can drive others away. They go to others as a source of support whenever possible and often cry to seek attention and support. They tend to indiscriminate self-disclosure. They are commonly in conflict with others as they complain that others never give enough; they feel chronically undervalued.

Because preoccupied individuals are very demanding they often view their friends as unreliable or insufficiently supportive or available. They can feel chronically exploited. Their friendships are enmeshed and conflicted. However, to preoccupied individuals, romances are usually the highest and critical priority and this often causes conflict with friends. This conflict can take many forms: ignoring friends when in a romantic relationship, using friends to manipulate a romantic partner, or viewing friends as potential sexual partners or as competition for sexual partners.

They may worry about never finding someone to share their life with but are likely to have been constantly involved in romantic relationships and after a break-up are likely to become immediately involved with someone else. They often 'fall in love' almost immediately and tend to idealize relationships, often to extreme proportions.

Their relationships are punctuated by emotional extremes, including anger, passion, jealousy, and possessiveness. They are more invested in the relationship than their partners and more dominant. They are clingy or dependent, and very demanding of their partners. The dominance and intrusiveness of the preoccupied is often reflected in an extreme desire to be needed, to look after, or to 'fix' romantic partners. Finally, preoccupied individuals have a hard time breaking off relationships, and will often stay in very bad ones.

DISMISSING: Positive self-model, negative other-model

As you will now know, I see an understanding of this attachment style as being of particular importance for working with men.

Key features: minimizes importance of relationships; high self-confidence, avoidance of intimacy and compulsive self-reliance.

Dismissing people do not talk about relationships. They come across as cool (or cold and arrogant in the extreme), matter of fact, unemotional and aloof. There is a striking absence of introspection and realistic evaluation of their relationship experiences though they may present a highly intellectualized relationship account.

When confronted with problems or upsetting matters, dismissing individuals distract themselves from their emotions, minimize the importance of the problem, and actively avoid going to others for support. Dismissing individuals are not emotionally reactive or expressive and rarely cry.

Dismissing individuals have a positive self-model. They have a moderate to high sense of self-confidence. When asked what others think of them, they may reply that others see them as obnoxious, aloof, arrogant, smart, argumentative, critical, as a smart ass, serious, or reserved. They are likely to say that they 'don't care' what others think of them. These individuals tend toward emotional independence (i.e. they are compulsively self-reliant). They tend not to be jealous nor to be anxious when separated from significant others.

Dismissing individuals have a negative other-model. They give the impression that they don't like other people very much (e.g. 'A lot of people are not worth getting to know'). They are usually cynical and very critical of others. They are cool and maintain an emotional distance from others. They are uncomfortable with affection. They are low in proximity seeking, actively avoiding going to others for support. They are particularly unlikely to cry in front of others. As one patient said, 'There's no way I'd let anyone know I'm vulnerable.' They engage in low self-disclosure with others and avoid interpersonal conflict. They stress the importance of independence, freedom, and achievement.

Dismissing individuals may describe their friendships as fine but, in fact, their friendships tend to be superficial, being founded primarily on mutual interests or activities rather than emotional closeness. They are happier when discussing the concrete world or activities and one of the most striking aspects of the friendships of dismissing individuals is just how low is the level of disclosure. They prefer not to go to their friends for help or support. As with the secure, the dismissing may be more or less outgoing and extroverted; it is the emotional connection or intimacy that is lacking.

Predictably, the romantic relationships of dismissing individuals are characterized by the same lack of intimacy or closeness, low self-disclosure and emotional expressiveness. These individuals are less involved in the relationship than their partners. They tend not to express affection and prefer to avoid emotional displays. As well as not relying on their partners for support they are uncomfortable with requests for support or indications of dependence in their partners. They often shy from commitment and are quick to feel trapped or bored in relationships yet are rarely on their own – there is usually some sort of involvement, however casual. It should be noted that many dismissing individuals are in long-term romantic relationships; again it is the approach to and quality of these relationships, rather than their presence or absence, that is critical.

Many of my male patients meet most of this description. Most of them have a default position that whenever there is a problem in a relationship they threaten to leave and never return.

It is important to point out that this four-category model con-ceptualizes working models that are more or less consciously held, though in fact they tend to operate automatically. All my clinical experience shows that, unconsciously, prototypical dismissing individuals do feel negatively about themselves, and their adoption of a detached stance toward others is a way of defending a fragile sense of self from potential hurt by others. Similarly, the positive other-model of the preoccupied masks a less conscious negative model of others, with the tendency to idealize others acting as a defence against acknowledging that significant others are, at least at times, uncaring and unavailable. Naturally, the idealization serves to defend against the underlying and deeply destabilizing feelings of hatred towards the idealized object. The apparently contradictory self and other models of the dismissing and preoccupied can be understood in terms of Bowlby's conception of multiple models.[8]

See Bartholomew[9] and Bartholomew and Horowitz[10] for further discussion of the prototypes. My thanks to Kim Bartholomew for permission to draw on her work in their description.

5
Sulking, Masculinity and Attachment

Almost without exception the men with whom I have worked have one of two common problems: the conviction that they were never given enough of the breast, or whatever the breast stands in for (such as maternal love), and they were all afraid of their father however much they might also have loved him. Many have both of them. Those of you who are taken with analytic ways of thinking will see the connection immediately. Here we have the most common problem we deal with in our patients – ambivalence and the positive Oedipus complex. It is the combination of the desire for the mother and the fear of retaliating attack by the father. There are two other convictions held by all abusive men: one is that their parents made too many demands; the other that they were never loved enough. I will return to these.

One of the most significant aspects of the Oedipus complex is that it signals the child's entry into the social world and begins the complex process of shaping his gender, his sexuality and his desires. From a preoccupation with the two-body relationship the child is confronted by the social reality that his mother has an intimate relationship with the father. The two-body suddenly becomes three-body – the most unstable of all social geometries. There are, however, early precursors of this threesome, located more in the boy's fantasies but still presaging his later struggles with the passions of the Oedipal triangle. The most obvious of these early versions is the threesome represented by the child and his division of the breast into the good breast and the bad breast

– surely the origins of all splitting. I imagine that it is already clear that I do not subscribe to the Kleinian notion of innate envy being the origin of this primitive split. Although I have always been attracted to attachment theory I have till now reserved my position somewhat with regard to the origins of destructiveness. I am now firmly convinced that the origins lie in the real inadequacies of the primary carer in the 'fit' with the child and its temperament, not in nature or innate fantasy or phantasy; more, I hold that the ferocity of the bad breast – and later fantasies about other people's hostility to one – is a direct correlate of the intensity of the frustrating or traumatizing experiences the child has. While there is much that I am not fond of in Kleinian thinking, I find myself in total agreement with its description of the process of rapprochement. Although it is not a developmental theory, and would not claim to be, Klein's description of the move from the paranoid/schizoid to the depressive position[1] is a major developmental move. The paranoid/schizoid position describes the internal world as being in a state in which objects (not necessarily people as anyone who remembers John Cleese, in *Fawlty Towers*, beating up his car with a tree branch will appreciate) are split into parts and separated from each other. In essence the bad object dominates and is perceived to be hostile, persecuting and dangerous and has to be split off from the good object in order for the infant to survive. The depressive position describes the internal world as being in a state in which the object (mother) is not split into parts but is seen to be whole. The good and bad parts are no longer split apart with the good object being idealized and the bad object denied. Objects are seen to be one and anxiety is depressive and focused on the fear of loss of the object through its destruction by the subject. This position is the beginning of guilt and concern and the object is preserved through the spreading or inhibition of aggressiveness. This allows for the stable introjection of a secure object, one which is not threatened by the subject's aggression. You may see how important this is in the context of the process of psychotherapy or analysis as the patient discovers, repeatedly, that the therapist is not destroyed by his/her destructiveness and can be 'taken in' over time as a secure object for the patient, one which can be used and will provide resilience for dealing with life's difficulties after the analytic process is terminated. Once developed, the pathways from the paranoid to the depressive position are there for use throughout life as we struggle with the primitive impulses and derivative anxieties left over from our inadequately parented early years.

The split necessitates some process of rapprochement with the carer to enable the child to continue to relate and receive the nourishment required for further growth and development. Without this rapprochement life may turn out very bleak indeed. My clinical experience, and my experience of men generally, is that very few men reach anything approaching complete rapprochement. It would seem that we are all left with some unresolved sense of injustice and its correlate, paranoid thinking. This sense of injustice is, I believe, largely responsible for the developmental failure which I have come to think of as the masculinity which enables men to abuse the women to whom they are attached and, in some cases, any other women. In my earlier publications I have made it clear that I believe all men grow up with this sense of injustice, that it is structured into the maturational process and the development of masculinity. Of course it varies in intensity from the mild to very severe according to the actual environment in which the child is raised and the extent of the real abuse, neglect or deprivation. I do not believe it is innate although I do regard it, to some extent, as inevitable. What then does a sense of injustice consist of?

The sense of injustice, splitting and sulking

Sulking is based on a sense of injustice, the belief that one is being, or has been, unfairly treated. That same sense of injustice when combined with learned masculinity, is responsible for most of the interpersonal violence we see in the world and certainly underpins the violence inflicted on women by men.

Subjectively, the sense of injustice derives from the experience of never having been loved enough, at best, to that of having been actively abused and traumatized at worst. Often the feeling is not so differentiated but is the experience of having been dealt a bad hand or that life has treated and is continuing to treat one unfairly. Along with the sense of injustice come feelings of frustration, sadness, fear and rage connected to the perceived source of the injustice. Hubris is often the result with all the attendant self-righteousness and self-destructive behaviour which this can entail. The unfairness (injustice) which begins its life in the two-body relationship with the primary carer, is not, in my opinion, symbolized or articulated as such until the Oedipus complex reaches its apogee. From this point on, the child is able to articulate questions that have been thought but unknown and on the basis of its new-found knowledge is able to write its own history. There is nothing unusual in this; the present has no history – history belongs to the future. The deep sense of frustration which I believe is part of the heritage of all little boys (see my *Why Men Hate Women*) is finally open to symbolization and interpretation and the sense of injustice can begin to take root. As the boy develops, he will see many roots of the injustice. From a psychodynamic viewpoint these will all, with the exception of real and substantiated abuse, be seen as a version of the castration complex, whether it is loss of the breast (weaning), birth of a sibling, separation and individuation, anal struggles for control and self-mastery or awareness of the father's relation with the mother. Of course these days it is difficult to differentiate real and 'unreal' abuse. As a result of changing fashions in child rearing and successive moral panics about child sexual abuse since the early 1980s we are, now, all victims. This change in fashion and the gradual awareness of the real scale of child abuse speaks to the problem of whether it is possible to take an attachment theory approach to psychodynamic psychotherapy. It is ironic that the problem which so troubled Freud at the end of the 19th century should so preoccupy us at the end of the 20th and the early 21st.[2] Not, however, that the presence or absence of 'real' abuse makes a great deal of difference when dealing with sulking. Psychodynamically, the task is the same in each case. It may be difficult for those steeped in orthodoxy but it is very important, when working with the sense of injustice, to acknowledge that a real injustice occurred but, equally naturally it seems to me, one has also to do this where there is no evidence of real abuse. In such cases the injustice is an existential one or a social one derived from, for example, fashions in child rearing or the construction of the patients' masculinity derived from the models available in the family of origin or in his local culture. There is always a subjective truth in the sense of injustice. Unless this is acknowledged there is little hope for change in the patient.[3] The therapist simply becomes another one of 'them' and potentiates the injustice by refusing to acknowledge that there is one in the first place. As we shall see, the task is to help its owner see that the sense of injustice is a facet of his character requiring constant dramatization. (See Chapter 12, 'The Function of Drama'.)

A great many of the men I work with have been abusive to a woman during their lives. Many come to me because they are actively abusive and those who aren't have almost always been unwittingly abusive (not violently) at some time in the past. It was the repeated discovery of this controlling, dominating and abusive behaviour in men who presented with other problems which eventually led to my establishing The Men's Centre, offering dedicated treatment for abusers, in 1984. As you may know, I came to the conclusion that being controlling and abusive is almost a default position for men in intimate relations with women and that this led me to a paradigm for understanding and helping men which differed from the analytic orthodoxy and from what I regarded as post-modernist confusion and uncertainty.

In the course of many years spent working with abusive men and applying what I was learning from them to my work with non-abusers, I came to the conclusion that sulking can be so intense that it is a clinical condition, most likely already subsumed under one or more diagnoses of personality disorder, but actually deserving of differentiation (see my *Men Who Batter Women*). In many men it is a sub-clinical or pre-morbid condition only too easily evoked with some intensity under appropriate circumstances.

Sulking is both a description of a state of mind and a set of behaviours. The aim of a sulk is to invite the perceived source of the injustice (always another person and usually, though not invariably, the primary attachment figure) to approach and make good the injustice, to make reparation for the damage they have caused. However, if they respond to this invitation the sulk will reject them. Sulking is an invitation to approach solely for the purpose of rejecting the approach. This process can be repeated until the sulk feels that the injustice has been righted, i.e. that the suffering is equalized, or until the victim of it has had enough and stops making approaches.

When I wrote about sulking in *Men Who Batter Women*, I indicated that I believed sulking should be recognized as a clinical condition. In a subsequent radio debate with a well-known psychiatrist from the Maudsley Hospital, he said that not once in his career as a consultant had one of his juniors told him that someone had just been admitted with a very serious sulk. I chose to ignore the rather obvious attempt to put me down and humiliate me (incidentally one of the main reasons why men are violent to each other and to women) and made the obvious point that the main reason for this is that sulks more often than not end up in prison, not hospital. They are more disturbing than disturbed. On the rare occasions when they end up in hospital the presenting symptoms would be of high anxiety/guilt and depression with mild paranoid features.

In *Men Who Batter Women* I located sulking midway between the paranoid and depressive positions which I described earlier. The paranoid position is seen by Kleinian analysts as a product of the child's phantasy life. It derives from innate envy and destructiveness being projected into the object and then feeling persecuted by that now destructive object. The experience is internal and has nothing to do with external reality. As I made clear, my own position is diametrically opposite to this. I believe that the destructiveness of the object is real and not simply the product of the infant's own projected destructiveness. For a brilliant account of how Freud misunderstood this in his famous analysis of the Schreber case see Morty Schatzman.[4] Any rage or anger the child feels, which may well be projected into the split-off bad object and thereby make it even more frightening, may be a healthy and appropriate (I will not say innate) response to the failure of the object/primary carer to respond appropriately to the infant. This lack of appropriateness in the carer's response can be experienced by the child as an attack insofar as any pain is experienced by the child as an attack on the self – including bodily pain. However, this should not obscure the obvious – that becoming a person is for most of us a painful process as we confront and surmount – or not – the developmental crisis which this necessitates.

The infant, naturally enough, wishes to attack the persecuting object (let us call her, for the sake of simplicity, mother) and this is clearly a desperate dilemma for the child given that the breast or mother which causes the pain is also the breast or mother who is the source of nourishment and love and protection. This is the origin of the splitting of the mother (and the world/environment) into good and bad, loved and hated.

The paranoid/schizoid position names the infant's manner of dealing with the relationship with the bad object. The object is experienced as containing homicidal impulses towards the child and the defences employed against it are primitive in the extreme. Of course it may be true that the object wishes to destroy the child. Which parent has not, at some time, experienced intense rage towards their children? In the Kleinian paradigm the origin of this is in the child himself and becomes a product of the parent through the child's projections and projective identifications. I believe this is mythical, not real, and that the internal bad object is both a reflection of the real badness of the primary carer (the first external object) and the child's aggressiveness. Apart from that I find the Kleinian description of the paranoid and depressive positions entirely plausible as an account of how it is that we all come to terms with the limiting and frustrating qualities of the external world and finally relinquish our unhealthy narcissism and reach rapprochement. I believe the route to this is sulking. A sulk is a position in which the infant is overwhelmed with a sense of unfairness or injustice about being hurt and the hurt itself. Additionally, he is filled with strong destructive impulses and a wish to retaliate and inflict as much pain as he feels has been inflicted on him. He cannot yield to the impulse to retaliate as he is sufficiently afraid of the damage he might cause and the fear of losing the object; nor can he articulate the pain he is feeling for fear of being subjected to more. In effect he holds both the paranoid and the depressive positions in his mind at one and the same time and is aware that the object is both needed (but not necessarily loved) and bad and hated. Donald Meltzer called this needed but not loved object 'the toilet breast' – an accurate and pithy name! The sulk is an elegant solution in that it enables its subject the expression of both his hurt and his vengefulness whilst providing the opportunity to equalize the injustice by repeatedly rejecting the object's attempts to repair the damage. I believe this is the route to rapprochement. In a positive process the sulk will experience fear of causing too much damage to repair, then guilt about damage already caused and ultimately concern and ruth for the object.

What then is rapprochement? I have already said that I believe it is crucial to reach a rapprochement with the bad object if one is to be able to reach emotional health and maturity. My clinical experience conforms to what Klein led us to expect. When there is a sufficient regression in the transference that it becomes negative and the therapist or analyst becomes the problem, not the solution, the treatment process is in prime position. In my view this is what therapists should be aiming for in every long term treatment; to enable the patient to regress to the paranoid/schizoid position in order that we can support the move to guilt, concern, remorse and reparation. In very favourable cases we may even receive gratitude. I know that David Malan's research did not support the idea that interpretation of the negative transference was essential for a good outcome in the analytic therapies.[5] In fact his research indicated it may be associated with not good enough outcomes and be a negative experience for the patient. I can only say that when I have been fortunate enough to help someone to this point the outcome has always been positive. However, it needs to be said that I have not managed this with all my patients. Also, it has always emerged in relation to effective work with breaks in treatment and the slow and patient dismantling of the resistances to the strong anxiety and passions that these arouse. At the outset these are inevitably denied. In my youth I would attempt to achieve this with plunging interpretations and they invariably failed and for obvious reasons. The old adage 'interpret the resistance/defence before the impulse' still holds good. To it I would only add, ensure that the resistance/defence is worked through before going to the impulse. This can usually be achieved by simply naming the defence and coupling it with the underlying anxiety before going on to mention 'unacceptable feelings or thoughts' or some other undifferentiated or non-specific and unthreatening state.

The usual process around treatment breaks is that the patient becomes anxious and depressed and will commonly act angrily with other people in his life in a way which seems inappropriate or excessive. Separation anxiety is universal and is probably the most painful of all anxiety. Often the patient will say something to the effect that if I know how much they are suffering then it must mean I do not care, at best, or am sadistic at worst. They reason, much as a child will reason, that if I know how much they suffer when they are left I could not leave them unless I wanted them to suffer. This is the paranoid position and if it is not handled well the therapist can find himself with some free hours after a break as they act out their destructive fantasies by withdrawing from treatment. The desire to let you know how painful it is to be rejected and abandoned can be very powerful.

Rapprochement is the process by which the child learns to accept the reality of the object mother/environment as being less than perfect but crucially as being 'good enough'. This entails developing a capacity for metabolizing disappointment – the experience of the mother/environment not coming up to one's expectations – perhaps the most painful of all emotions. This is the beginning of the development of psychic muscle and the capacity for affect regulation.

Of course, this process cannot begin unless the sulk is dissolved sufficiently for the man to begin to acknowledge that he has an attachment to the therapist. This can prove to be extraordinarily difficult to achieve as it runs counter to some fundamental qualities of the big M. You will not be surprised to learn that men revert to the security of the big M during times of perceived threat that replicate the original traumas of separation and individuation. I remember David Malan telling me jokingly that the staff at Harrods got hell from customers during the six weeks of the analytic summer break. This was shortly after the long summer break in my analysis during which I had provoked a few incidents with people who I believed were 'failing in their duty of care' towards me. These incidents were quite unnecessary and my behaviour was quite out of character. They had involved my behaving in what I would now describe as a hyper-masculine way. The analysis was only possible after I had angrily sulked at him for longer than I care to disclose! The paradox of sulking is that whilst it may be obvious to the outside observer that the sulk is on and that it is a very childlike set of behaviours, the sulk himself can have the experience of behaving in a 'strong' way in that he is denying that the attachment has any significance and can be scornful or contemptuous of any attempt to suggest otherwise. I remember a patient laughing and telling me 'to get over myself' after one such attempt. As I have already said, dissolving the sulk and the hyper-masculinity is not really possible unless the sense of injustice is addressed and validated. It is not impossible to agree that an injustice has occurred when the world is seen through the eyes of an adult who has regressed to the age of a toddler. The key is getting through the aggression, whether it is overt or passive. I am not saying the rapprochement is reached only through the analysis of the transference around breaks in treatment but they are a major contributor to the process. If we understand attachment as perhaps the most basic instinct and separation anxiety and anxiety about loss as the most basic anxieties then it is easy to understand why this is so. However, whilst it is true that not all men suffer from attachment disorders or if they do are comfortable in so being, it is also true that all perverse/deviant/controlling/abusive men are dismissive/detached and regard this as a marker of emotional maturity rather than a counter-phobic and defensive position.

I hope that I have managed to sufficiently unpack the connections between sulking, attachment and masculinity. I fear a complete unpacking would require a separate book. However, these considerations lead me directly on to those situations where affect regulation is ineffective and splitting and the paranoid/schizoid position combine to produce destructive outcomes.

6

The Domino Theory – The Root of Masculine Destructive and Self-destructive Behaviour

There is an apocryphal story in the work I carry out with male abusers. It is commonly referred to as the coffee cup scenario. It is based on an actual incident and I frequently recount it in groups to a lot of laughter, both wry and shamefaced.

The real incident involved one of the very first men I ever treated for violent abusive behaviour. At that time my colleagues and I were much concerned to eradicate triggers to violent outbursts – believing that if we could do this the violence would stop. This phase of my professional development took place after my personal epiphany into a pro-feminist model of understanding masculinity and abusiveness but prior to the realization that there was no such thing as a trigger to violence – only events which are subjectivized as precipitators by perpetrators who are looking for a reason to be violent (there are many who are beyond the point of needing a rationale).

However, this man – let us call him Andrew – had finished his supper and his wife had just finished clearing up after the meal and had put the children to bed. He was sitting watching TV with a cup of coffee as she finished her daily chores. After all, he had already done his day's work – it finished the moment he walked in the door at seven that evening. He had spent a cursory 20 minutes with the children whilst he waited for the final touches to his supper.

She announced her intention to retire for the night – understandably tired with three small children to care for. As she was leaving the room she had said to him 'Please put your cup in the dishwasher.' Andrew replied 'What?', in what he later described as a 'normal' tone of voice – certainly a different tone from hers which he described as hostile and provocative. That his tone was normal in his interaction with her was not in any doubt – nor that it was extremely threatening and hostile.

Jenny, as we will call her, repeated herself with what would certainly have been an added note of anxiety in her voice. Andrew sprang up and out from his chair and screamed at her, 'You're never fucking satisfied with anything I do are you?' He stormed past her into the kitchen and the next thing Jenny would have heard was the loud sound of shattering glass as he threw his mug through the kitchen window. She retreated upstairs, no doubt fearful for her and her children's safety. She had been through this many times and it had usually resulted in her being physically assaulted by Andrew. The retreat was to provide only temporary respite however. A few minutes later Andrew burst into their bedroom in a splenetic state, clearly enraged and looking to impress it (actually 'inflict' would be a better word) on Jenny.

Well, impress, inflict he did. For the next half hour he harangued and abused her, firstly emotionally and finally hitting her until she collapsed weeping on the bed. Only then did he stop. The content of his torrent of abuse mainly concerned how much of a victim he was. That it did not matter how much he did, how hard he worked, how much he gave of himself or his time or his money, she always wanted more because she was never satisfied. The evidence of her dissatisfaction was her constant demand that he do more – the coffee cup and the dishwasher being the obvious example. Why could she not leave him alone just to enjoy a quiet moment at the end of the day without imposing a final demand on him.

If there is any man out there reading this who says he cannot understand what Andrew is saying then I will say you are either mendacious or self-deceptive. I don't ask that you identify yourself with his abusive treatment of Jenny, but simply his perception of the unfairness of his domestic circumstances.

There are important questions raised by this vignette and they relate to what I call the 'domino theory' of violence. How is it possible for Andrew to get to physically abusing Jenny because she asked him to put his cup away? Moreover, how was he able to feel so abused himself, which he patently uses as a justification for abusing her and the children? What precisely does it all mean? I could use any one of hundreds of examples to illustrate the domino theory – another very common one concerns those situations where a woman indicates that she is unhappy in some way – the content is unimportant. The consequence is that she ends up being abused for being unhappy and the content of the verbal abuse is uncannily similar to the content of Andrew's abuse of Jenny.

The domino theory is taken from the American phrase used to justify the wars in both Korea and Vietnam. The theory had it that there was an axis of communist evil spreading from Russia in particular and in these cases from China. The prevailing wisdom had it that if any of the satellite states in Asia were to fall to communism it would spread around the whole region. Military logic dictated that it had to be stopped in its tracks wherever it first appeared or each neighbour state would fall successively under the influence of communism.

So it seems to be with abusive men. Of course we are not talking about neighbouring states, but a complex series of interlinked emotions and attitudes and belief systems concerning self and other. In what follows, it may seem that I am in some way endorsing the idea of triggers to abuse. However, this is not the case. In saying that it all hinges on the first domino of the man's interpretation or perception of the precipitator – in this case the

request to put the mug in the dishwasher – I am explicitly saying
that it hinges on his interpretation, not reality. To put it bluntly it
hinges on the degree of his paranoia and this will need to be defined
– the paranoia that is. I will go further. I believe that the process
about to be described underlies most forms of destructive and
self-destructive acting out by men whether infidelity, gambling,
risk taking, visiting prostitutes, overworking etc. and that these
are attempts to work out the anxiety occasioned by the underlying
shaming and humiliating experience.

In cases of violence – all violence excluding the utilitarian
criminal form in pursuit of financial gain – the dominoes, the
emotional ones of which are what comprises sulking are:

1. Disrespect
2. Not feeling appreciated or loved
3. Injustice
4. Anger
5. Shame – humiliation
6. Intense desire/imperative to avoid shame – easiest through
   violence
7. Unfairness – basic injustice – narcissistic in quality, at not
   being loved/feeling lovable – connected to narcissistic shame
   about this
8. Abuse/violence, self-destructive behaviour

As I pointed out above, non-abusive men will frequently resort
to other forms of acting out to defend against anxiety connected
to their unacceptable destructive feelings and impulses and to the
unbearable underlying shame – the forms of behaviour described
in the Introduction and which are so stereotypically masculine.

Disrespect

So in Andrew's case the first domino was the request from Jenny.
For Andrew this was a disrespectful demand or instruction/

order. He felt she was talking down to him or treating him as a subordinate. He went to some lengths to justify this perception but the fact was that he felt this way whenever he was asked to do anything by a woman except if he was attempting to seduce or flirt with her. He also felt persecuted because they had had many arguments about his not pulling his weight in the household chores. These were all evoked by Jenny's request. He actually felt guilty about what he knew to be the truth – he did not do his fair share. He knew he should do more but his experience was that he felt so tired by his working day that he did not want any extra demands made on him and furthermore felt that she did not have the right to ask for more from him as he was already fulfilling the major role of a man: to provide.

From his guilt he projected hostility into Jenny's request. He over-attributed malice to her tone and her intent. It may have been that she had felt some hostility when she had made the request but certainly not so much as Andrew then experienced. All abusive men over-attribute malice to their partner's behaviour. This enables them to escalate their behaviour without conscious guilt and to attack and punish the woman in an attempt to teach her not to do what he does not like. It is a simple conditioning technique – and all the more effective for being random (should he attack her this time or not?), and partial (how much punishment should he inflict?).

Not feeling appreciated or loved

From his point of view it is clear from her hostility to him that she is not acting from a feeling of love or respect. On the contrary she is acting from anger or even hatred. Does she not know how hard he works, how he sacrifices himself every day as he goes out into this difficult world in order to bring home the bread for the table, the house, the clothes, etc. etc. etc. Obviously what he contributes is not enough. If it were enough then she would not make these extra demands on him, particularly when he is tired and tense from a hard day at work. Or even more so at weekends when he is trying to repair the damage done by a hard week at work. In short she should never make demands. Of course if he wishes to offer to do more voluntarily he will do so and she should show true gratitude.

Naturally, all this means that she cannot possibly love him – otherwise how could she inflict such hurt and disturb his peace of mind?

There is of course a twist in the tail of this issue. We are all inclined, quite naturally, to blame others or external circumstances for any painful feelings. The feeling of being unappreciated is just that, a feeling. Whilst not wishing to discount reality I normally take the position that a feeling is an internal state for which the subject is responsible. Of course a state of arousal can be determined by external events, but the state and its constructed meaning are internal events and subject to the same interpretation as any other form of behaviour. I normally take the position that if someone feels unappreciated it is because he is incapable of feeling otherwise and that remedial action is required to enable him to learn how to feel differently. It is not possible to 'feel appreciated' if one does not appreciate oneself – i.e. believe in one's lovability. No amount of positive feedback will fill the hole of low self-esteem – it is simply an analgesic for the pain of feeling unlovable – a narcissistic supply. Of course I believe a permanent solution to this is best achieved with a psychoanalytic/dynamic approach in which the process of developing and resolving the transference plays a major part.

Injustice

The sense of injustice is a natural for this situation – it follows as night follows day.

He works hard. As far as he is concerned everything goes into the family. He is the provider – and we know from research that men prioritize their role as provider over all others, whether father, lover, etc. Considering he gives all it surely isn't too much to ask that his needs should sometimes be given priority over his children's or his wife's. Surely it is simply gratuitous provocation for her to ask him to stack the dishwasher before he goes to bed? Quite simply it is grotesquely unfair. Of course you may argue that such language (grotesque) is inflammatory and that I should not be using it. The point is that he does, and worse in his head.

I have written extensively about the origin of the sense of injustice in men and its close connections with what is commonly known as male paranoia. When abusive/violent men present for treatment one has to pay particular attention to the sense of injustice. I shall say more about it in general soon, but want to preface that with the way in which it is presented by men and how we might interpret it during the assessment and treatment process. In essence it can be collapsed into three different sources in the way men talk about it although they are all usually far from the unconscious truth of its origins. Basically men will say that they are angry and feel unfairly treated (sense of injustice) because:

- she does not give him enough
- she demands too much
- she does not appreciate him/his efforts, does not love him, loves someone else, rejects him for another etc.

I appreciate that it could be seen as rather simplistic but it is not difficult to construct these as being expressive of oral, anal and phallic/Oedipal developmental issues respectively. I take refuge in the fact that this way of framing the issues provides important insight into the level of fixation of the man concerned and therefore as a rough guide to his developmental conflicts. Each of these represents a narcissistic wound of a particular kind although it is no guide to the depth of that wound or his dangerousness without supporting data about actual events in his childhood. After working with violent and domestic offenders for almost 30 years I am in no doubt that there is a relationship between early privation and abuse and the level of risk a man poses to others. Additionally, my hypothesis is that the more regressive the level of fixation the deeper and more profound the sense of injustice the more severe are the defences and the potential big M or hyper-masculine behaviours – crime in particular. It follows from this that the more regressive the sense of injustice the less effective ego/secondary process functioning is available and the greater the difficulty in resolving his dangerousness.

The man will locate the origins of his feelings of injustice in these issues because they are easily identified and lend themselves to dramatization and enactment. Its true origins are neither so accessible nor so easily dramatized (although it is not impossible to do so). The point is that a sense of injustice requires a persecutor or it makes little sense. The allocation of this role to an external object allows for many possibilities which pre-empt disturbance or undifferentiated distress.

Anger

This leads him (indirectly as we shall see) into a feeling of what may at that stage be an undifferentiated state of distress/arousal which gets structured as anger – but is more likely to become infantile rage. He has no insight into what is going on, but this feeling of injustice and the accompanying anger/rage are unconsciously connecting to a very ancient source of precisely these feelings and the beliefs associated with them. If he were able to take a moment to reflect, or more importantly were motivated to, he might differentiate the distress into the feeling of injustice and the helplessness, vulnerability and lack it speaks to. However, for a large number of men this is impossible. The pain and the lack, the vulnerability, the failed attunement and dependency are simply overwhelming. Affect regulation is not normally practised by abusers – except outside the home where it usually involves suppression rather than thought, containment and working through. Anger seems the only recourse and it possesses the added advantage of filling him with feelings of potency and power – the very opposite of impotence or helplessness. Of course there has to be a point of identification for this anger unless we simply assume it is nothing other than an innate or essential response of masculinity (a position I am not comfortable with for obvious reasons). Do we need to look any further than the father of the primal scene or the Oedipal father of fantasy with his retaliatory, castrating rage in response to the little boy's challenge to his dominance and his ownership of the object of the little boy's desire – mother? As I have already made clear, an angry father is neither an essential nor sufficient condition of a little boy growing up to be angry or violent. Culture provides enough sources of identification for this to be unnecessary. I might add that I do not believe this will ever change so long as men go to war and the nation state requires a masculinity which is capable of killing, maiming and raping in its commission. You may be familiar with the saying that 'men are capable of feeling anything so long as it's anger'! It seems that abusive men are inclined to construct any state of undifferentiated arousal as anger and this may be true for many men whether or not they are abusive.

Shame – humiliation

Alongside the anger (I have ordered these feelings sequentially although I doubt this is accurate as I will show later) Andrew experiences an intense feeling of shame and of being humiliated which has been present since he heard the first request concerning his coffee cup. This derives from what Jim Gilligan[1] refers to as being disrespected or, as many men would have it, 'bitched'. This unfortunate terminology has great power in work with men, even though it is hard to imagine anything more sexist in origin. In the high security forensic units in which Gilligan worked it referred to the experience, very real, of men attempting to dominate others in the system. The ultimate form and expression of this dominance occurred when one man became another's bitch. This meant he was a sexual possession, to be available at any time to provide sexual pleasure for his master. This also included being made available to other men who wished to use him for pleasure and who were willing to pay for the privilege. Gilligan has shown that men will go to any lengths, including risking their lives, to avoid this fate. Often their masculine pride (phallic narcissism) is all they have left in forensic settings. As they see it, the loss of this final prop to their collapsed internal world renders life meaningless. Of course we can see that what we are describing here is phallic narcissism and the ultimate threat to it – castration. Of course the castration is symbolic; the receipt of another man's penis into the anus or mouth effectively reduces one to the status of a woman, another castrated object. It is experienced as an attack on a core self construct – one's gender identity as masculine. This potentiates the fragility of masculinity – actually a hyper-masculinity which forms the basis of the entire ranking system in prisons – how tough are you? Often one's pride in one's toughness is the only source of self-esteem for many men denied any opportunity to thrive or be productive in their lives. This hyper-masculinity requires close examination. Like all hypers it is an excess and in this case it is an excess of those qualities which in certain sub-cultures pass for signifiers of masculinity – but as a hyper it is predicated on its opposite. It is intended to conceal the fact that the man does not feel masculine (as he imagines that might or should feel) and that all masculinity is predicated on castration.

I realize that I expose myself to charges of exaggeration by this unexpected comparison between men who abuse women and anti-social personality disordered prisoners (and, by implication, all men).

Men who will risk their lives in prison in order to pre-empt the symbolic castration or to regain their masculine status are sufficient evidence of the significance of shame in male psychology and the lengths to which men will go to avoid the experience of shame and public humiliation – and the collapse into failed phallic narcissism. Of course this phallic failure is profoundly connected to the more basic narcissistic wound, where it exists, of the experience of not being lovable, what we refer to as self-esteem. One cannot overestimate the degree of suffering experienced by hyper-masculine men.

To balance this description of shame defences in hyper-masculine men I will give an example of a more normal equivalent in a fairly normal session in my practice.

This concerns a highly intelligent and ambitious young man who had initially been referred to me for treatment because of homicidal feelings towards his infant son. At times these feelings were acted out in a most disturbing way and tested to the limit my capacity for containing anxiety for the child's safety. He never reported doing anything that inflicted physical harm to the baby, although it was clear that this may have been more a matter of luck than judgement.

He arrived for his session one day carrying a full tennis bag slung over one shoulder. They are big. They are also ungainly and require to be carefully negotiated around corners and through doors. The door to my rooms is of standard size. At the beginning of his treatment Michael, as I shall call him, usually charged around regardless of what he was doing. He was hyper-active or hypo-manic. As he attempted to negotiate his bag around the doorway he banged it into the frame of the door. No physical damage was caused, either to the door or to Michael. The havoc

wreaked on his psychic frame was another matter. He slung
the bag to the floor and himself to the couch and proceeded to
indulge himself in a rant, for this is the only word which would
do it justice, against himself and his incompetence. En route he
took in what a waste of time and money was his treatment. I was
a wanker, he was a wanker and he deserved anything destructive
which might befall him. He hated his wife and his son. His
treatment was not doing him any good at all, he was just as
angry and destructive as he had ever been and he still could not
win at tennis – incidentally the arena where he played out most
of his Oedipal transference in stories of how he could not beat
players who were not as good as him. The swear word count
must have been in the hundreds and it was impossible for me
to intervene. Any attempt to do so brought forth more invective
about my incompetence and general impotence. Fortunately the
rant blew out before the end of the session and we were able to
begin to reflect on what had happened. Although it had not been
mentioned during his rant, I was sufficiently familiar with him
to know that the precipitating event had been the collision with
the door. How is it that such a simple error of judgement could
lead to this outburst of destructive rage and invective towards
himself, others and the world? He was a keen sportsman and his
reaction to losing was to launch a vitriolic attack on himself; he
would break equipment and shout insults and profanities loudly
enough for his opponent to hear. He was completely unable to
give credit to his opponent, believing that he should always win
regardless of the level of skill of the opposition.

There are a number of things you need to know about this
man which might cast some light on this behaviour. He was
narcissistic; painfully preoccupied with his appearance. He
was always conscious of how others might see him as if he
was constantly on camera. Naturally he was very judgemental
about the appearance of others and quick to denigrate those who
did not meet his exceptionally high dress code. Obviously his

obsession with his appearance and the feeling of being constantly under observation derive from processes with which we are familiar; a lack of any real self-esteem and a belief that he was not worthy of any sort of attention so that the fantasy of being watched was a grandiose, wish fulfilling fantasy. It will come as no surprise that in his fantasy the watchers were not simply admiring. If they were women they desired him and if they were men they envied him.

His mother had been a very beautiful professional model and the walls of his childhood home were adorned with large, blown up pictures of her. She had divorced her husband when my patient was under five years old. She had also been a bully and frequently hit my patient as well as never missing an opportunity to shame or humiliate him in front of friends or family members. During his early teens he had become a great fan of spy stories of the James Bond variety and had decided that these men, Bond in particular, represented a model of masculinity which he was determined to imitate. This was no idle identification! As he grew older he was prepared to spend large sums of money buying the clothes and other items of dress that Bond favoured. He also admired his taste in cars and his treatment of women, seeing them both as possessions that reflected his value as a person.

What became clear as we analysed his outburst was that such clumsiness was a total contradiction of everything he aspired to; he felt deeply ashamed at having bashed the door. It subverted the image he wanted me to have of him – as 'perfect' – and betrayed his real and flawed self. It spoke directly to his underlying and profoundly low self-esteem and all the narcissistic rage and shame associated with that wound. This incident shows how, for men, aggression is a readily available defence against shame – it demonstrates his power and belies how small, impotent and insignificant he feels.

So to recap. The connections run in this way:

The unfairness – the basic injustice – is experienced as narcissistically painful, damaging to the 'self' or identity, by which I mean the sense of masculinity overlaying the earlier constructed fault line derived from the dis-identification with the mother. The experience is of not being loved/feeling lovable – this is connected to narcissistic shame – the absence of self-esteem. Self-esteem is the basic belief that one is worthy of love.

In the prison population, where feeling 'bitched' is intrinsic to the shame and humiliation of incarceration, it is also a further threat in the struggles for power within the prisoner population. It is not hard in these circumstances to see the real source of the present shame. However, even this requires some analytic explanation as to why shame and pride should be of such primary importance and why so much significance is attached to 'loss of face'. The loss of face signifies that one is no longer worthy of the respect of others – to be held in esteem by them. This speaks directly to the original source of the shame – the belief that one is not worthy of respect or love. That, in fact, one is not lovable. This is the most shame laden belief of all – that one is not good but in fact is bad. This is not innate. To the extent that such a belief is held by a person then to that extent it has been placed in her or him by his early carers who have failed to provide an attachment which the child experienced as protective or secure. In some cases, certainly with prison populations, this will have been an actively damaging attachment in which the vulnerable child was traumatized by emotional, physical or sexual abuse.

This maltreatment will leave the child with all manner of problems, many of them potentially life threatening or emotionally disabling.

What ties all these complex emotions and behaviours together is the sense of injustice. What then are the origins of the Sense Of Injustice? It derives quite simply from the experience of having been unjustly treated by one's original carers. The world – parents that is – actually owes babies and children a living in the sense of a chance for life. The injustice is that many men (also women but that is not at issue here) have been denied that chance and indeed offered its antithesis – seemingly a chance for destructiveness and death – what Schatzman called Soul Murder.[2] Injustice is, of course, a relative concept. It would seem that every child believes that what he gets is exactly the same as other children.

Masculinity offers the little boy some opportunity to escape the shame of being unlovable. This is the real power of the Oedipus complex – standing as it does like a distant beacon of integration and wholeness – the chimera of phallic promise; an oasis of desire in a desert of love. I will look at this in the next section. Let us return to the domino theory.

When Jenny asked Andrew to put his cup in the dishwasher what he heard was a reproach – you do not do enough. This translated into her not appreciating what he does, and what he does is not insubstantial, however feminist you are. To put it bluntly, it is unfair. Now I know that to all you adults out there, the idea of a fair life is the preserve of paranoids and children. In most men what we see is a potent combination of both. To potentiate this are all of Andrew's chauvinistic attitudes, beliefs and feelings that as a man he should not have to do housework anyway. After all, he goes out to work. His job is to provide – hers is to care, in whatever ways he stipulates a woman should care. So when she makes her request she is treating him like a woman – this is basically disrespectful. In the language of the prisoner he is being 'dissed'. This amounts to emasculation – the symbolic castration. He is being bitched and feminized. (I would be failing in my duty if I did not mention, in order to elaborate it later, that the woman who he experiences as bitching him has, in effect, assumed the role of a man. She has become the phallic woman – the early fantasy of which plays such a central role in Oedipal drama in little boys and which evokes his most powerful anxiety, castration anxiety.) It needs to be re-iterated that although shame has its origins in earlier experience, the phallic narcissistic construction of masculinity is, from an analytic viewpoint, essentially a defence against what men know to be true. That we are already castrated and that the Oedipal experience is an experience of phallic failure converted into triumph through identification with the fantasy of the phallic father at whose hands we experienced this defeat. The mediating object between the defeat and the identification can only be the exciting pleasure-giving erect penis with which we have wanted to possess mother. In this way Freud's statement that 'the ego is first and foremost a bodily ego' is, so to speak, given flesh. The little boy identifies himself, his body, with the penis and its qualities – potency and aggression being the most apparent. (Might it be going too far to suggest also that one of a man's secret wishes is that the phallic woman might use hers on him?)

As I pointed out earlier, it is interesting that men construct their narratives of abuse around Freud's three phases of sexual or libidinal development as it progresses through the oral, anal and phallic/Oedipal periods. It may be that these constructions unconsciously mirror their real development although what we can say with certainty is that they reflect consensually constructed narratives of female failure so far as men are concerned.

For men, work is love made plain. So if she does not appreciate the work he does – it is not enough – then in effect she is saying that his love is not enough. Enough for what? one might ask. In essence it is not enough to pre-empt the attack which he experiences she is inflicting on him at that moment and which he translates into confirmation that he is, at best, more bad than good and, at worst, simply bad. Of course he is over-attributing malice to her. The over-attribution of malice is standard for abusive men, or indeed for men who are aggressive in any situation (look at the average road rage incident – always predicated on the projection of malice). The fact is that he needs to over-attribute malice in order that he can experience his overwhelming sense of injustice – the injustice he has lived with all of his life and is never able to understand or articulate. He is condemned to re-enactment and acting out in a compulsive attempt to work it through and mitigate the anxiety and metabolize the grief and rage. Impossible.

It needs to be said that with many men, not only the abusive and violent, it will prove difficult or even impossible to identify such a clear injustice in early infanthood as having been given the message that he is unlovable. Where it is clear these men are more likely to be found in the secure institutions into which they have unconsciously manoeuvred themselves in order to get at least their most basic dependencies met without having to acknowledge that this is what they are doing. After all, they are locked up because they are a risk to society, not because they are needy and frightened and unable to cope with the demands of everyday living. Abusive and violent men who have not yet managed to get this degree of caretaking or who do not need it and who present for treatment will in any case have available to them, as they have grown up, an easily identified menu of sources of injustice from which to choose.[3] This menu is the one described earlier as deriving from oral, anal and phallic/narcissistic sources. Attitudes and beliefs derived from these are reinforced during the development of masculinity by the adoption of perceptions of femininity and femaleness which describe it in derogatory, devalued and contemptible ways. For a fuller description of this I refer you to *Why Men Hate Women*.

Perhaps the crucial point about the sense of injustice which needs to be constantly reiterated to men is that it is as much a quality of theirs as their shoe size, their hair colour or their height. As I will later explain in Chapter 12 ('The Function of Drama') such an intense feeling requires a drama, acting out, in the attempt to find a solution to the pain and the hope of redemption through triumph over the persecutor. A man with a sense of injustice needs to find or create persecutors as a means

Precipitators	Dominant trauma	Responses	Behaviours
Perceived unfairness/disrespect Demands Failure to live up to expectations An angry woman Any slight or criticism	**Phallic** (Oedipal, three person)	Castration Shame Humiliation	Phallic-narcissistic masculine: • Violence/aggression • Infidelity • Pornography/masturbation • Prostitution • Alcohol • Gambling • Risk-taking • Overwork murder Sulking suicide
Any stress – e.g. work Frustration Alienation Vulnerability	**Pre-phallic** (Pre-Oedipal, two person)	Low self-esteem Reproach You're bad Your love is no good Your love is bad You can't love You're not lovable Neglect Abuse/trauma	Breakdown and regression: • Helplessness • Passivity

Figure 6.1 Schematic of the connections between perceived injustice, shame, pre-Oedipal trauma and phallic narcissistic masculine behaviour

of rationalizing or explaining his chronic dis-ease and to provide him with a rationale for acting destructively. Within the drama he knows why his interpretation of the world makes sense – it provides him with all the legitimacy and validation he needs.

Some special precipitators

There are three major precipitators (I stress that these are not 'triggers' as they are commonly thought of in violence literature) of the sense of injustice which require special treatment when unpacking men's motives for self-destructive acting out or abusing women and they are intricately connected. They are the birth of children, the demands this imposes on the man and the envy of the child for fulfilling the man's deepest wish, which is his desire to use a woman (his partner) as an object in exactly the way his child is using her. The connections are apparent although the need and desire to use an object will require some theoretical unpacking. There is no time in life when more activity is expected of people in relationships than when a child is expected and born. Feminists have long made the point that men's treatment of women is fundamentally abusive and controlling, and that it should not be regarded as a pathology. There is a great deal to say for this, none the least of which is that it's true! The vast majority of men who abuse women or, more usually, control them, are not psychiatrically ill. However it has become abundantly clear to me, after many years of working with violent offenders, that a very large proportion of them suffer from some form of personality or developmental disorder which is psychodynamically diagnosable whilst not being an illness as such. As we have seen, the question 'why do men want to control women?' requires a complex answer from an analytically trained practitioner. From a feminist who has no clinical interests and who sees the issue from the perspective of gender politics, the answer is deceptively simple. Men want to control women in order to ensure servicing and guarantee its provision in the future and punish for failure to provide it when required. They (we) want *to use an object*. What this means will become apparent.

Actually, the complex analytic answer and the apparently simple feminist one converge as we shall see. Research shows repeatedly that men, when asked, regard their role as providers as being of paramount importance in their marriages. There's nothing particularly surprising in that you might say. That is what men have done for thousands of years and it is deeply embedded in culture and in definitions of masculinity and manhood. My clinical experience is that non-abusive men share this same perception as abusers, but abusers take it a step further and regard it as their only role in marriage. As far as they are concerned, once they enter the home after a day or week at work that is it. They have done their bit and have no further duty. They symbolically throw the carcass to the floor and retire to the corner of the cave for R and R and to await the presentation of the finished meal. This does not necessarily mean that they are unwilling to perform any other tasks, such as child care, but it does mean that other tasks are optional extras, not duties. Whether or not they perform any other tasks is entirely within their discretion and control and this is not open to negotiation or discussion. Within the home he is supposed to be king and his female partner is supposed to reward him for all his efforts in providing life's essentials. As one man expressed it, 'away goals count double'. Isn't this what he has learned about boys and men and girls and women since he has been old enough to understand the difference? Fundamentally we are educated to expect servicing from women and this covers all aspects of life from feeding to fucking and, not forgetting of course, washing and ironing. Interestingly, it seems to me that the abusive intensity of these expectations, and the sanctions for failure, kick in after the decision to have children. It is tempting to postulate that the expectations arise only because women give up working outside the home when pregnant or after giving birth but the fact is that the vast majority of women who work for money outside the home also do the vast majority of the household chores. The basic rule of his rule is 'don't expect anything of me over and above providing for you'.

What of the connection between childbirth, the social construction of masculinity and men's abusive response to demands? Imagine the situation of a man who has been enjoying the exclusive attention of his partner and they have both been earning salaries. Imagine, two incomes, no kids and no demands. If they are living together it is likely that she has been taking care of the home and him also. He is the centre of her world, always in her mind (at least he can imagine so). They decide to have a baby to complete their union in the fantasy that they are adding to the relationship and that this baby will be the symbol and concretization of their love for each other. He may notice that her preoccupation with the baby begins while it is still in the womb. In favourable circumstances they will have many things to do together to prepare for the baby's arrival, and there is much she will be doing alone in the privacy of her mind as she develops her attachment to her unborn child. It is at this point that many men begin to abuse; I call it The First Child Syndrome.

7

The First Child Syndrome

Over the years I have come to believe that men's difficulties (including violence) with women should be headed off at the pass; prevented rather than cured. This sprang from my growing awareness that many of the men I was working with had first begun to behave badly or abusively when their partner had become pregnant or given birth. I think what I am about to describe is true for a very high proportion of men – including non-abusers. I suppose it is testament to one of the central issues about childbirth that it took so long – almost 15 years – for this awareness to crystallize into a specific idea to mitigate and prevent the problems with which I was dealing on a daily basis; and in most cases far too late. This central issue I refer to is the social and cultural denial of the sheer difficulty of being a parent and, for a man, a father whilst trying (needlessly, I might add) to preserve the relationship which led to the conception in the first place. It has to be said that this is not something that most men are very good at. Another element of the denial is that men are not told that the chances that their primary relationship or attachment will survive are not much better than even and that such as do survive do so in a radically different and unrecogniz-able way. What nobody tells men (I think women are told or know in some visceral way) is that children are not fun. They are bloody hard work. It can be relentless, draining and unrewarding in the short to medium term except in short patches. It takes all your resources to do it well enough – all resources from money to feelings and goodwill. The man goes from being top of the feeding chain, so far as he is concerned with his partner, to the bottom. He is therefore relatively deprived. At the same time he is required to provide more in the way of all resources to enable the mother and child to have a good enough start to the child's life. In addition it is unlikely he will be thanked for his pains. On the contrary it is likely that he will feel constantly reproached by his partner for not doing enough, not giving enough and not appreciating enough how difficult is her role in looking after an infant for 24 hours a day. Of course I am using some hyperbole here. However, there are many men, including psychotherapists, who will resonate instantly with this extreme scenario. As professionals they will also recognize in this the seeds of many marital failures and crises.

During my career in working with men I have consistently observed how the discovery of a pregnancy and the birth of a child can seriously disturb and in some cases fragment a man's personality. In a very short time an apparently stable person can become unbearably anxious and depressed to the point of experiencing suicidal feelings and impulses. There are many reasons why this should be so. What is transparently clear to me is that in the main it is because men are not prepared for pregnancy and especially for becoming fathers and parents. In addition, it is easy with hindsight to see how many of the marital difficulties presented by men can be traced to the birth of their children. These difficulties are not faced and therefore not resolved. They sit like an untreated wound in the centre of the marriage. They cannot be acknowledged and therefore faced because the source of them is not permissible for men in what is supposed to be a time of joy and celebration – bringing a new life into this world. I vividly remember an old friend of mine (a successful and essentially very good person) sitting in tears in my home as he described to me how he did not want the second child his wife was now pregnant with. He was in a state of intense fear, guilt and depressive anxiety which made no sense to him. He was struggling with suicidal impulses. It made great sense to me but I was not, nor did I want to be, his therapist. I simply listened to him for a while and suggested that he take a risk and discuss his feelings with his partner. He did this and his anxiety diminished to manageable levels. Their child was born and I watched her grow into a delightful young girl who had experienced being truly wanted as a baby. I want to emphasize that this man is a normal, non-neurotic, highly successful and good hearted human being. What might such a crisis have precipitated in someone more challenged and without the same support system? What I want to do in this chapter is outline some of the main anxieties men have to face and show their origins and the consequences of not facing them.

We know from published research that the first pregnancy and the year after the birth is a difficult and fragile time for couples, the new baby and the marriage itself. Some researchers have discovered that this is the single greatest event time in which men inflict abuse on women. It is also the period when the beginning of most marital failures occurs, if not necessarily the failure itself – and not necessarily with the birth of the first child. It can occur with the birth of the second or third or later children.

I remember one man, P, in his late 20s who came to me after he began to beat up his wife during their second pregnancy – the first child was one year old at the time. He was overwhelmed with the injustice of his situation. He was giving more and more both of his time in helping around the house, shopping, cooking etc. and in working harder to earn more money now that his wife was unable to carry on her career as a teacher. She no longer seemed interested in him, their sex life had diminished to almost nothing; she never cooked meals any more. In fact all she seemed to do was reproach him for the inadequacy of his contribution. His sense of the unfairness was overwhelming. He would spend sessions railing at her inadequacy as a wife and mother – in his opinion she was far too close to the children. At times it was impossible to get him to stop and hear the awful things he was saying. He was frankly paranoid at times and believed that his two year old daughter wanted him out of the house and was colluding with the wife to achieve this. She did this by not being affectionate enough!

Sadly, I was unable to prevent P from acting out sufficiently to make his presence in the home safe for his wife and children. I instructed him that I would be unwilling to work with him unless he moved out. Surprisingly, he did so and took his old room in his parents' house. It became clear that he had been struggling since the first pregnancy. His abuse of his wife had started then, although he had not been physically violent to her during that pregnancy. That started with the second. As we began to explore his history he remembered his difficulty when his younger sister had been born and how rejected he had felt by his mother. His sister had potentiated this by rejecting him too, as he saw it. It was difficult to help him to see that maybe his physical maltreatment of her (including one frank attempt to kill her by pushing her pram, with her in it, down a flight of steps) might have had something to do with her nervousness around him. His bullying of her had never ceased whilst they occupied the family home until he left it, and her, in his mid 20s.

The transferences (by which I mean the unconscious projections onto his wife and children) in such a situation are not unusual, although they are very complex. There is no doubt in my mind that his wife came to represent his pregnant mother and that his children represented his younger sister. Unconsciously, of course, his wife had represented his mother prior to her first pregnancy.

We continued our work together with him living out of the marital home. He maintained contact with the children, although having moved out when the baby was only two months old he really could not develop any form of attachment to her nor her to him. The separation did not go well. Soon after, he met and began a romantic attachment with a young woman. He grew increasingly distant from his wife and children and fairly soon had effectively lost contact with them. This was a very sad story although the outcome was undoubtedly the best, in the circumstances, for the children. He was simply unable and unwilling to do the work he needed to do to repair the damage he had done to the relationship. In essence his sense of injustice was simply too powerful for him to give up his sulk and his hubris. Justice (and being right) was for him more important than his relationship with his wife or being involved in the raising of his children. I could tell this story many times over. It is a story of men's ill-preparedness for partnership with children. P's story (and it became a very sad one insofar as his children, at last contact, have not seen their father for over six years and are unlikely ever to know him) is typical of many of the men I have worked with. We have already seen how the sense of injustice develops into abuse and violence but what I want to explore here is how this sense of injustice is very often precipitated by pregnancy and birth and what are its vicissitudes apart from violence.

For many of the men I am concerned with, pregnancy, whether planned or not, is experienced as an acutely anxiety provoking experience. If a man discloses a plan to have a baby or a pregnancy we underestimate the intensity of this anxiety at our patient's peril. What we know about anxiety is that it is one of the most unpleasant experiences a person can have. Most of us will do anything to relieve it. It is anti-life and anti-pleasure. It is not uncommon for people to believe that being prepared for the new baby is a function of having purchased the cot and the clothes, getting the room ready, etc. However, preparedness has little to do with these practical issues. It is fundamentally about being emotionally prepared to receive the helpless arrival and to absorb its impact on the entirety of one's existence.

Much of the anxiety of being prepared for the arrival is displaced onto gathering together the practical resources needed for a new baby. However, being truly prepared involves the gathering of internal, emotional and psychological, resources.

The simple fact of the anxiety this arrival will precipitate is that, on the face of it, men will often adopt extreme measures to cope, measures which are dysfunctional and destructive for the marriage and the well-being of children. The most common of these measures, which are intended to prevent the slide into guilt, depression and crippling anxiety, and which can occur before and after the birth, are:

- overwork
- alcohol
- gambling
- pornography and masturbation
- infidelity
- abusive behaviour
- withdrawal, uncommunicativeness
- sulking
- loss of sexual interest
- visiting prostitutes
- compulsive spending or other manic behaviours
- suicide
- self-destructive behaviour at work
- hyper-masculinity, aggression, road rage, violence

It is worth pointing out that the purpose of this book is to understand why men do these things in any case. Reactions to fatherhood exemplify and amplify those behaviours – pregnancy throws into sharp relief the problems with masculinity.

The superficial origins of the anxieties are relatively simple to understand. As already mentioned, he has to adjust to a situation where he has to provide much more not only to his partner but also to the new baby whilst he feels he is getting less and less – the breeding ground for a potentially overwhelming sense of injustice. This is very dangerous as it is the root of righteous anger and violence. The tasks he faces in order to muster the required internal resources are myriad. He must face up to the powerful, unresolved anxieties connected with his own childhood and his own experience of being parented. He needs to come to terms with any feelings of jealousy he has towards his newborn child and his feeling that he has lost his partner and any associated desire he has to be rid of the child as he might have wished to get rid of his new siblings.

He faces the difficult task of metabolizing his feelings about being the husband or partner of a mother. We need also to take into account, in his efforts to do this difficult work, the extent to which he is subject to cultural pressures to behave in a 'manly' way and not be open about anxiety or depressive feelings for fear of being shamed or humiliated by his peers.

And this is not the end of what is required of him whilst he struggles to maintain his integrity and do what is necessary as the father of a newborn. His dominant models of a couple and parenting will have been formed during the man's childhood and he will have an internal model of a couple with a baby which is based on his perceptions of his own parents. His internal model of a father will be his own father.

These internal models may be functional or dysfunctional. They need to be unpacked, elaborated and updated. His perceptions of his masculinity will undergo a real challenge after the birth. Parenting is a feminizing experience for many men and they cannot cope with it. This can result in some hyper-masculinizing of his own behaviour – again defensive and potentially destructive.

As I write this I am again shocked by the task facing men and that it has to be coped with without any preparation or training. More preparation is required of them if they wish to drive a car on public roads and for most the demands are simply too much. Even when they stay within the marriage it cannot be without recourse to some of the strategies mentioned above for coping with such overwhelming anxiety. Often this will create a schism in the marriage which is irreparable.

Why, then, in this extremely demanding time in his life – in which high levels of anxiety are averagely expectable – does a man indulge in the forms of acting out enumerated above?

The first and obvious answer is that they help him to cope with his anxieties. The second and slightly less obvious one is that each of them enables him to feel powerful in the face of overwhelming feelings of helplessness. They provide him with the feeling that he is in control and they bolster his fragmenting sense of self by bolstering his unravelling sense of his masculinity – his coping, his strength, his toughness and independence, his potency. In short his phallic narcissism.

Paradoxically, even acting destructively to his partner will achieve this same end – even if temporarily.

It may begin with verbal abuse as she finds herself unable to care for him in the way she did prior to the pregnancy. It may be violent abuse as he tries to 'beat the life out of her', as one of my patients once expressed it to his partner and as many women's organizations describe it. Either then or after the birth, his experience is that he has moved at least one step down the affection or feeding chain (the baby has also stolen her breasts from him – metaphorically or actually), so he is getting less in terms of care from his partner; at the same time there are more demands on him to provide care as she is preoccupied with keeping the baby alive and he is required to provide for both of them in order to secure the environment emotionally and physically. The emotional/care equation becomes massively out of balance from his point of view and his resentment may become proportionately unbalanced. Add to this any unresolved sibling rivalries and the situation is explosive. The way he copes with his growing resentment and the underlying helplessness, impotence and fear will determine whether or not he becomes an abusive man or is able to commit to a relationship and stay in one when the going gets tough – as it always will. Many men will begin to feel *used* at this point. Expressions such as 'she's taking the piss', 'she's exploiting me', she's using me' are common as the man articulates his sense of injustice. What these represent is his ineffable experience that his desire is being frustrated and that she is doing to him precisely what he wishes to do to her and which the child is doing in his stead.

8

The Use of an Object

The desire 'to use on object' was first expressed in Winnicott's original paper, 'The Use of an Object and Relating through Identifications', published in 1969.[1] In my opinion this paper rates with Freud's 'Mourning and Melancholia' as one of the most important in the psychoanalytic canon. I hope my use of it does it justice. As I understand it there is a phase in the infant's emotional development when the infant effectively destroys the object with its savage excited treatment of her (the breast). Of course, at this stage the infant has no awareness that the object is separate from him. He effectively attacks the object in the selfish pursuit of satisfaction – the baby at the breast can be seen to feed with almost savage and excited intensity and has no care for the welfare of the breast. As soon as the infant is satisfied the breast has effectively been destroyed in the service of the infant's satisfaction – it ceases to exist. The miracle is that the object/breast/mother is miraculously resurrected the next time the infant is in a state of need or desire. The infant does not possess the capacity to endow the object with an internal world or needs and desires of her own. The miracle is that the repeated destruction of the breast/object followed by its repeated resurrection, at the point of need or desire, establishes the object as indestructible and therefore available to be used secure in the knowledge that it will always be there – this is what Winnicott calls object constancy. It precedes the development of guilt or concern for the object and the entry into the paranoid/schizoid and depressive positions and the ultimate rapprochement – she is there simply to be used. She exists only to gratify the infant's desires. The theoretical and developmental implications of this are manifold and fascinating. However, what interests me here is how these are expressed in adult masculinity. The majority of men I have worked with, abusers and non-abuser alike, have related to women in precisely the way Winnicott describes the infant's relation to the object prior to her establishment as an object available for use – prior to object constancy. Of course there are differences of degree, but in essence she is related to as if she is simply an extension of the self or a projection of the self.

In the extreme, she is not believed to have a mind, her opinions are worthless, her beliefs are irrelevant, her needs are unimportant, her desire is threatening and therefore denied. In short she is there to be used and ignored when not needed. Many abusive men take it almost as an affront when their partners insist on being acknowledged in elementary ways such as being allowed to refuse to have sex, or to have sexual desires of their own. The default position of men is NO! whether or not they are abusive.

I will take a liberty with Winnicott's use of the word 'use' of an object which is rather idiosyncratic. I will employ the word in an entirely opposite way to his meaning. For him 'use' was a synonym for 'relate'. For me it is the opposite of relating and describes more the sort of behaviour prior to the establishment of object constancy and the object's availability to be used.

Men will experience a sense of injustice and outrage whenever a woman refuses to be used as an object or behaves in a way that rejects and refuses her status as an object and insists on her subjectivity. It is almost as if he believes he is being denied his birthright and his sense of injustice matches the injustice he feels is being inflicted on him.

In my opinion this is the root of all men's desire to control and dominate women and the cause of the difficulties men have in relationships. It is impossible for a woman to satisfy the man's need to use. Prostitution and pornography are about as close as it gets without actual enslavement, but they are pale substitutes and require a large dollop of suspension of disbelief and appreciation of reality.

Are women the same? I believe so, but the desire is buried beneath many layers of socialization into unselfishness, submissiveness and compliance. However that is a different book.

What is apparent is that men are bigger and stronger and more permitted to employ punishment, intimidation, aggression and violence when frustrated or disappointed. If women wanted to use their partners as objects and attempted to do what men do when confronted with their failure, i.e. punish them for the failure and simultaneously train them not to disappoint in future, I suspect that many more would suffer more extreme violence than do now. Is it any coincidence that in times of war the uses to which women are put by invading armies are almost indescribably brutal and that their destruction is not symbolic or fantasized but often all too real? I will return to 'the use of an object' (with my definition of use as meaning narcissistic relating) and its relation to violence shortly.

Although it is crucial in understanding and treating domestic abuse to address the sense of injustice, it is equally important in addressing all forms of masculine acting out, not simply aggressivity and challenging behaviour. Without acknowledging the injustice, pride and hubris will prevent any psychological or behavioural change. For those who have followed my argument this far it should be clear that I have gone further in saying that the sense of injustice has played a major part in the development of most men and masculinity itself.

The problem is that the sense of injustice has both universal/ structural and idiosyncratic sources as I have already indicated.

To all this it is essential to add the crucial ingredient – masculinity. All of the factors above would apply, perhaps even more, to women. However, they do not become violent and abusive to their male partners nor, in the main, do they indulge in the acting out of the activities outlined on page 100. Of course they lack one essential ingredient – the phallic narcissism so central to dominant, controlling masculinity or simply masculinity itself. Masculinity is the cornerstone of the structural/universal origins of the sense of injustice. It derives its importance from its pivotal role in the origins of and determining effect on the politics of gender as defined by the institution of patriarchy. Any attempt by women to frustrate what a man believes are his rightful expectations derived from patriarchal definitions of manhood and womanhood will evoke a profound sense of injustice relating to his feelings of castration or emasculation. That these feelings are so pivotal derives from the even more determining location of phallic narcissism in masculine development. Then there are idiosyncratic ones connected with all the orthodox explanations outlined earlier and based on early environmental failure. I believe it is these which potentiate the structural ones and add the element of dangerousness. For the moment I have said sufficient about phallic narcissism but will return to it later.

The sexualization of frustration and the use of an object

One cannot write about men without referring to frustration. Every man I have ever met struggles with very high levels of it. Actually, frustration is an empty category. Manifestly, it refers to unfulfilled desire. However, desire is also an empty category – and socially constructed except for eating and sexual expression (also probably genderless or object neutral). I believe that the basic frustration relates to the inability to make meaningful contact with the other. However, whereas Otto Kernberg[2] believes this to derive from primary envy I see it as attachment related and derived from attachment hunger and the failure to use an object. I also believe it to be potentiated by the unfulfilled desire for justice, which at the very least requires to be acknowledged and validated and, at the extreme, will not be satisfied without revenge. It is a state of alienation and psychic isolation. I believe that most men who are in positions of power and authority suffer from insecure attachment and profound frustration. Many practitioners who want to help men deal with this frustration, particularly those who offer 'anger management' are wedded to the frustration theory of aggression and to the idea that anger rooted in frustration is responsible for men's destructive acting out. Apart from anything I have said earlier about acting out, it is not difficult to deconstruct and disprove this particular hypothesis. Firstly, if abuse derives from frustration why is it not randomly expressed rather than being consistently inflicted on the same target? Secondly, why do the vast majority of abusive and frustrated men demonstrate a capacity for containing frustration in most other areas of their lives and in other relationships except that with their partner? Thirdly, why is there an assumption that frustration leads to aggression? It might, and does with many women at least, just as easily lead to helplessness, depression and anxiety. I could go on with this deconstruction, but will not except to make a final point that is often made by women who have been abused. Anger, they say, is not a *cause* of ab/use; it is a *form* of ab/use. There is no gainsaying this observation; ab/use is in the eye of the victim not the perpetrator. Granting the perpetrator of any crime the right to define his own behaviour simply hands him another and more deadly form of abuse. The notion that violence is caused by anger or frustration may be culturally acceptable but that affords it no more veracity than if it were expressed by Islamic terrorists. (For the sake of completeness and to nod towards those men who actually are victims of abuse by women I will simply add that misogyny is not a justification for misandry. Just because many men attempt to pathologize women's reactions to maltreatment does not mean there are no pathological women.)

That said, this analysis does not free me from the necessity to incorporate frustration into my theory of masculinity and particularly its connection with violent and abusive behaviour and other forms of acting out.

It is a commonplace that men sexualize their frustration. I don't think many people appreciate just how common this is. I remarked in *Why Men Hate Women* that an erect penis seems like the answer to a child's anxiety about his unresolved dependency needs because for the first time he has in his own hands (so to speak) a source of pleasure and satisfaction which belongs to him and him alone and which he alone controls. It is hardly surprising that this connection between fondling his penis when he is distressed or excited should be carried over into adulthood, although actually I think the situation is more complex.

The model I propose is based on my understanding of events that occur during, especially, the pre-Oedipal period of development. However, I am convinced that the groundwork for these has been laid earlier in culturally prescribed ways of raising boy children compared with girls.

After analysing thousands of episodes of hostile behaviour, aggression and violence and an equal number of masturbatory fantasies and perverse behaviours I have reached the conclusion that men's adult capacity for experiencing frustration – and this varies enormously – is fundamentally derived from their early experiences of having dis-identified with the mother and adopting an insecure/detached attachment style – detaching from – the mother or primary carer and the subsequent attachment hunger which this creates. In *Why Men Hate Women* I discussed the defence of converting trauma into triumph in masturbatory fantasy (see also Chapter 12 'The Function of Drama', below). The dis-identification, the detachment, occurs when the boy child is beginning to experience his deepest passion for his mother and also beginning to experience genital excitement. In this cauldron are the elements needed for a life of fantasized and sexualized triumph. Sexualization is established as fundamentally a defence against the depressive feelings resulting from the attachment failure and the loss. This gives more flesh to Stoller's assertion that sexual fantasy is an attempt to manage pain and trauma by converting it into triumph.[3] In my experience this is always a motive. This is the nodal point to which men will return for the rest of their lives as masturbation is used to ward off pain and anxiety.

The important point about this dis-identification and detachment is that much of the thwarted attachment gratification is physical – it is the desire to hold and be held. This is made all the more intense by the child's increasing sexualization of his attachments during Oedipal development.

'The ego is first and foremost a physical ego,' as Freud remarked. I believe that insufficient physical care in the form of touching and holding bequeaths a deep well of longing and an incapacity to feel held or touched, both really and metaphorically. Naturally this also includes powerful negative feelings, of anger or rage (or later constructed as such), directed towards the frustrating object – the primary carer. To the extent that the much earlier relationship during infancy has been a failure there is an increasing likelihood that this will lead to a man's needing to control women in order to pre-empt further frustration and pain – the more so as the earlier failure establishes a developmental platform in which need, anger and rage are conflated. If the control fails, abuse and punishment are a simple escalation.

This is the basis of the construct of 'toilet breast' in which the object is needed and not loved but is hated and envied. It also gives rise to the need for all workers with men, whether abusive or not, to understand the 'need to use an object'.

As I said earlier, Winnicott describes a very early phase of development during which the object (the mother/breast) is repeatedly destroyed by the infant as it satisfies itself. This does not mean aggressive destructiveness or innate rage or hatred but rather intense eagerness and excitement like eating when very hungry. It is ruthless, lacking in concern for the object or guilt about the phantasized destruction from which the object continually recovers and which it survives – the breast is represented over and over again after having been internally destroyed. In this process, the object is not external but internal. It is entirely a product of the infant – it is a subjective object. This is a totally narcissistic phase of relating – there is no external world to speak of. Winnicott is concerned with the move from this narcissistic type of relating where objects are projections or extensions of the self to a more advanced form of relating where objects are recognized as separate and distinct from the self. This requires the establishment of what he calls object constancy. Quoting from Winnicott's 'The Use of an Object and Relating through Identifications', Donald Carveth writes:

> Winnicott is concerned with the process whereby the subject comes to place the object 'outside the area of the subject's omnipotent control; that is, the subject's perception of the object as an external phenomenon, not as a projective entity, in fact recognition of it as an entity in its own right' (p. 89).
>
> 'This change…means that the subject destroys the object' (p. 89), '…that after "subject (narcissistically) relates to object" comes "subject destroys object" (as it becomes external); and then may come "*object survives* destruction by the subject"' (p. 90; Winnicott's emphasis). He continues:

> 'A new feature thus arrives in the theory of object-relating. The subject says to the object: "I destroyed you." "I love you." "You have value for me because of your survival of my destruction of you." "While I am loving you I am all the time destroying you in (unconscious) *fantasy*." Here fantasy begins for the individual. The subject can now use the object that has survived' (p. 90; Winnicott's emphasis).

Finally, according to Winnicott:

> '*There is no anger* in the destruction of the object to which I am referring, though there could be said to be joy at the object's survival. From this moment, or arising out of this phase, the object is *in fantasy* always being destroyed. This quality of "always being destroyed" makes the reality of the surviving object felt as such, strengthens the

feeling-tone, and contributes to object-constancy. The object can now be used' (p. 93; Winnicott's emphasis).[4]

An essential point is that the 'destruction' of the object resides in its failure to survive without a change of attitude or quality. When the object does so, the infant learns that his eagerness, excitement or ruthless love is not destructive and that the object has the capacity to survive its own potential destruction.

My observation is that the unconscious reason for abusive men's intolerance of demands is that they have not successfully negotiated the phase of development in which they have learned they can destroy the breast (the mother/object) repeatedly and that she can survive the destruction. Like David Malan, I believe this is a consequence of the 'first exchanges going wrong' (i.e. she did not survive without a change of quality or attitudes) and that that eager excitement becomes real aggression and destructive impulse. Wanting their adult female partner to be a slave or servant is an adult version of this unresolved need and they have never discovered 'the otherness' (the subjectivity) of the object. It is almost as if she is a product of their fantasy. She exists without her own needs or her own mind. She has no subjectivity. She only exists when he is in her presence. If she challenges these largely unconscious, unthought and unknown beliefs and attitudes this can be profoundly confusing to the man.

The step from an ordinary man's failure to 'ordinarily' control the object to an internal system which justifies and legitimizes abuse and violence and an actual attempt to destroy her is a fairly easy one after years of socialization into sexism and chauvinism and learning that marriage is a licence to hit.

Of course these same circumstances occur in the lives of many little girls who, undoubtedly, develop into adult women with the same predilection for maltreating/using their intimate attachment objects. Manifestly, though, they do not become violent to men or women (although this does not preclude the possibility of a desire to control). The additional elements required for that particular outcome are particular to the development of masculinity. There is a clear connection between the failure of attachment and sexualized frustration and, I believe, men's propensity to sexual and sexualized violence. I have already explored (in Chapters 2 and 4) the well documented observation that a large proportion of men function from the insecure attachment style commonly known as detached or dismissive. It is also known that detachment or dismissiveness is a defence against the disappointment of the need for intimacy and dependency, the very needs which were originally frustrated. Although it is based entirely on clinical experience, I am convinced that men who masturbate to excess do so because they are unable to make a satisfying secure attachment within which they can experience sexual connectedness. Of course this begs the question of the meaning of 'excess'. I take it to mean a preference for masturbation within an available sexual relationship. Many of these men have no difficulty in accepting an appropriately timed interpretation, when they are discussing their lack of sexual satisfaction or frustration with their partner, that intercourse for them is masturbation *in utero*. The masturbation is compulsive of course. It is not practised out of any genuine sexual lack – although that may be also present – but out of a deep sense of disconnection, isolation and loneliness. In a word, depression. In fantasy these are mitigated and temporarily relieved – but at a price. Although it is pure speculation, we may say that if the research into the use of the internet as a pornography provider is accurate, the world is full of men who are struggling with depression and using pornography to self medicate by using the 'pornographic object' which is an entirely narcissistic construction. The easy and secret access to pornography has made it somewhat easier, in recent years, to access patient's sexual fantasies and masturbatory habits. No doubt it has also provided millions of men who would never otherwise have used it, for reasons of shame or guilt, with access to pornography.

As I pointed out in Chapter 4, it seems to be the case that dismissiveness or detachment could be considered the normal attachment style for men. In *Why Men Hate Women* I offered an explanation for this in terms of Ralph Greenson's argument about the little boy's need to dis-identify from his mother in consequence of which he disavows all tender, vulnerable and needy parts of himself, beginning with his infantile dependency needs and the associated need for a secure attachment. I am aware that the mental health industry has colonized attachment theory and that secure attachment is seen as a sine qua non of mental and emotional health. This was never intended by Bowlby. He was keen to stress that his theory was an evolutionary one and that attachment style is value neutral. It has only one goal and that is adaptation to the environment. However, I believe that we all yearn for secure attachment and that this need is innate. If unsatisfied it leaves a residue of longing coupled with grief and anxiety with which we will struggle for the remainder of our lives.

So, if we take the following...

- A failure to develop an object that can be used (in Winnicott's terms).
- Failed attachment or (more accurately) the establishment of insecure attachment. The beginning of attachment longing and its frustration.
- The failure to use an object and a failure to develop concern, guilt and reparative urges.
- The dis-identification with the mother under the sway of the phallic period and the development of the Oedipus complex.
- The denial of all qualities associated with the 'feminine' – primarily dependency, vulnerability and neediness.

- The discovery of the pleasure to be had from masturbation.
- The beginning of phallic narcissism and the masculine ego ideal.
- The failure of the establishment of the woman as separate other – but simultaneously constructed as object of desire and as a cure for frustration.

...it is not hard to understand how it is that men use sexuality in the polymorphous way we do and why sexuality is ultimately so subversive, harking back, as it does, to the most primitive and unresolved elements from which we are formed. From there it is transparently obvious why men should sexualize frustration and imbue it with such aggression in real object relations.

9

Phallic Narcissism Revisited – Competition, Aggression and Status

And this brings me back nicely to the central element in the above account – phallic narcissism. After a long career as a psychotherapist I believe I have finally understood the import of Freud's account of phallic narcissism. I believe he did not make as much of it as he might have in accounting for the development of masculinity, largely because he was given to understatement, but I am convinced that any practitioner who does not understand it simply fails to understand masculinity and maleness. If you don't understand phallic narcissism you don't understand men! Freud was very preoccupied with the resolution of the Oedipus complex and the phallic phase was a way station en route to that resolution.

I have my own understanding of the Oedipus complex and it differs in many respects from the orthodoxy. My own interest in it was occasioned by a remark of David Malan when he said that a great many of his male patients did not seem to have been through the Oedipus complex as it was understood and did not enact it in the transference. As therapists we are taught to look for and expect its emergence, not only in whole object triangular relationships but also early, primitive part object relationships.

The construct is so central to the development of masculinity that it is impossible to avoid tracing at least some of its history as an idea. The 'phallic' phase or stage of childhood development is thought to succeed the oral and anal stages and is 'characterised by a unification of the component instincts under the primacy of the genital organs'.[1] It is not regarded as the stage in which full genital supremacy is attained but is rather a precursor insofar as it is the beginning of the end of the Oedipus complex.

On its relation to adult genital organization – in which the sexual aim is genital coupling and reproduction – Freud had this to say:

> this phase (i.e. the phallic phase), which already deserves to be described as genital, presents a sexual object and some degree of convergence of the sexual impulses upon that object; but it is differentiated from the final organization of sexual maturity in one essential respect. For it knows only one kind of genital; the male one.[2]

This refers to the fact that the phallic phase is characterized by a belief, in boys and girls, that all people are possessed of a penis – so called universal phallic monism. Without this belief the Oedipus complex could not exist as it is the belief in the loss of the penis by the mother which ushers in castration anxiety and the final dissolution of the complex. This notion has particular interest for me considering the number of men I have met who either cross-dress or are particularly interested in forms of pornography involving pre-operative transsexuals. The latter are men who can live successfully as women and who still have penises although they often look and are, very (almost caricature) feminine.

It is during the phallic phase that the little boy directs narcissistic interest towards his penis. The great sexuality debate of the 1930s was centrally concerned with whether little girls also believed in the phallic monism of which clinical experience provides much evidence – or, as asserted by the grand dames of psychoanalysis,[3] they have an intuitive, innate, knowledge of the vagina which means the phallic phase is a defensive formation. I do not want to explore this issue in relation to girls but it is of great interest to me when thinking about masculinity and male sexuality. There is little doubt that phallic narcissism is the cornerstone of what I think of as the big M; masculinity as it informs the development of the masculine ego ideal; i.e. the kind of man we aspire to be. Masculinity is a phallic narcissistic construction. Understanding this is of primary importance in psychotherapeutic work. It has long been recognized that shame is a dominant affect in such work. Shame is connected to the failure to live up to the standards of the ego ideal; we 'let ourselves down'. As has been remarked before, although guilt and shame are closely related, guilt seeks confession, forgiveness and absolution whereas shame seeks to hide. This obviously has major implications for psychotherapeutic work.

It is believed that during the phallic phase the little boy identifies his whole body, from the top of his head to the tip of his toes, with an erect penis. What does this mean though? We have to imagine how a little boy might experience an erection. First and foremost I think we can assume it would be pleasurable and that manipulating it or fondling it would probably potentiate that pleasure. These pleasurable sensations would undoubtedly radiate through most of his small body as they do when most adults experience genital sexual pleasure. This pleasure is probably all the more intense if, as we might presume, internal bodily boundaries are not completely established. Parallel to this, there is incomplete differentiation of boundaries between the internal and external worlds. The remnants of this can often be seen in treatment of men with problems of perversion or some form of compulsive sexual behaviour or eroto-mania.

In Freudian theory, the exit from the phallic phase is occasioned by the little boy's recognition that those objects called girls do not possess a penis. This is the beginning of the onset of castration anxiety and the process of resolution through the development of masculinity 'proper' in the Oedipal phase. Proper insofar as it now involves another opposition – femininity. The crux of this is the recognition of the absence of the penis on girls and

women and the emergence of another opposition, that between
phallic/castrated. Implicit in all this is the development of the
notion of the female as inferior and what Freud described as
'normal contempt' for women. I want to make it clear, if I have
not already done so, that I believe Freud's account of the Oedipus
complex to be incomplete. For a fuller understanding I believe we
have to include in the account the father's jealousy and feelings
of exclusion from the intimacy between the child and the mother
– and I believe this is true regardless of the child's gender (see my
earlier comments on the roots of the feeling of being 'excluded'.
So the Oedipus complex is 'impressed' on the child by the father's
acting out of his own, unresolved, complex). In other words I
believe the complex is as much initiated by the father as by the
child and is not entirely the product of the child's fantasy. The
anger of the father may be real and explicit, as it was in the case
of the patient whose father had insisted he be sent to boarding
school at age six in order to 'make a man of him' and pre-empt
his feminization by the mother (what fathers of my parents'
generation would have called a 'sissy'). Little girls want a penis
so that they can 'have' the mother. Penis envy derives from that
particular failure (any sensitive father of girls will have seen this
in development) just as castration anxiety in boys is emblematic
of the failure to do the same. It is here that we can find the
roots of the defensive phallic construction of masculinity in boys
as they identify with the castrating all-powerful phallic father
created in their Oedipal fantasy. This identification expresses
so clearly what it is intended to deny – the symbolic castration
of the rejection by the mother and the real failure to defeat the
father with all the shame and humiliation this engenders. Again,
I ask parents to remember the rage of children when they face
defeat at simple games with parents. How many of us allowed
our children, boys and girls, to win in order to protect them and
ourselves, from the pain of that rage and shame? Of course I am
not blind to the obverse reality of the negative Oedipus complex

in which one can see these same processes at work in relation to the same sex parent.

I know many people scoff at the idea that little boys can make so much of their possession of a penis as to use it as the bedrock of their understanding and elaboration of the notions of masculinity and femininity. How can it be, they ask, that the source of so much fascination for men, female genitals, can be the source of the supposed trauma of castration anxiety? Why would men go to such extreme lengths to see, touch and enter the hypothesized wound? How can this wound be the object of so much interest if it is, indeed, frightening? This is not so difficult to answer. Apart from the imperative so much loved by biologists (which we have to admit is rather blind and probably is a simple need to penetrate any hole) there is also the need for constant reassurance that the wound has not happened to oneself. The compulsive need to put the penis to the test which I see in so many of my patients, is testament to the obvious fact that there is a feeling that it did indeed happen to them. The seduction and conquering of women speaks to the symbolic castration which has already befallen them and which underlies the fear of actual loss of the penis, a fear at its apogee at the end of the phallic phase. I might add to this the need of many men to attempt to heal the wound by filling it with the penis. However, I believe there is a more important motivation for men's denigration of the vagina in its construction as a wound. Is it not simply a clear example of the conversion of trauma into triumph? The vagina, whose possession was so passionately desired and so traumatically lost, has now become the sour grape of all sour grapes. In this way I believe, the vagina becomes the source of so much sexual confusion and anxiety, even fear, in men. I am aware that this construction implicitly hypothesizes castration anxiety as being as much a product of the Oedipus complex as its source. I would not be the first to construct such a hypothesis.[4]

I think there is a very simple operational definition of the phallic narcissistic construction of masculinity but before I approach it let me first say that I am aware that there may be many men for whom this operational definition does not resonate and to whom it may not apply.

In essence, the definition gives credence to the clichés and music hall jokes about men. Everything we do can be reduced to attempts to measure our potency against other men. Most male activity is generated by the need to demonstrate that we have the penis (although strictly speaking I should say the phallus) and that it is larger or, at the very least, not smaller than yours! Strictly speaking it is inter-subjective rather than narcissistic or is a secondary narcissistic phenomenon. In other words it belongs in the world of object relations. However, it is to be noted that the object of these efforts is other men, not women. I can almost hear the protests at this outline of (M)asculinity. In my opinion this is the bedrock of men's identity. I vividly remember a group in which the phallic narcissistic construction was being discussed – this is a frequent focus in the men's groups I conduct. It usually generates much humour along with serious reflection and interestingly, but perhaps surprisingly, disclosures are often accompanied by shame. I will come back to this. In this particular group the discussion concerned the cars the men owned and the relation to penis size (actually the inverse relation was the manifest concern). Comments were made about how they owned or wanted to own a car which demonstrated their potency or wealth and how they wanted to be the object of admiration and or envy to their peers. I made an interpretation that the envy they wanted was penis envy and that this was supposed to be the province of women. After a few minutes of this one man, who had remained silent during it, burst in with 'I'm not like that at all!'

This man was known to be rich. He was a retired property developer who had been quite successful prior to his early retirement. He was also extremely competitive in the group processes, displaying a need to be seen as wiser and somehow better than the other men in the group. When pressed by the group about his comment, he went to great lengths to tell us that he insisted on driving cheap and small cars to avoid just what the group was describing, i.e. the stimulation of admiration or envy in other men. What followed was a rather tense struggle with the group trying to uncover his phallic narcissistic displays and his becoming increasingly resistant to their efforts by pointing out how he wore cheap clothes etc. The group finally gave up and one man commented on how admirable this group member was in that he could resist the phallic display that was so obviously a compulsion for other group members. After a while a very perceptive member of the group laughed and said that he now knew how this rich man displayed – he did so by being better than all the other men in being sufficiently manly to resist the need to display his manliness with the size of his car or expensive clothes etc.

Our resistant member burst out laughing at this intervention and nodded his agreement. Pretending to be better than you really are in this way is a very subtle defence against the underlying (and in his case always apparent) need to be top dog. However, like all defences it also expresses the impulse against which it is intended to defend.

Another vignette from this same group gives some insight into some underlying dynamics in the competition.

The session began with one member saying he had been reading a book on assertiveness and it had made him aware that he had never been assertive in his life. He laughed as he told how, if he was being interviewed for a job, he would use every opportunity that presented itself to be self-deprecating and let the interviewer know essentially how useless he felt himself to be. Another member interrupted to say that he was also unable to be assertive because he was afraid of being rejected and he believed that assertiveness was a form of rejection which would invite retaliation. I thought about saying something about how this seemed to refer to the fear of being different from others and that in groups in particular the pressure to conform could be very powerful. The group seemed to be expressing anxiety about whether it was possible to be different in the group without being rejected. However, the group was flowing nicely and it seemed that my silence was the best thing I could offer at this stage. Another member commented that prior to his joining the group he had been unable to assert himself with his wife without being abusive. It is unclear to me what was said then (it included something about sibling rivalry), but it led to the same man disclosing that this (the previous comment) had been one of the reasons he had experimented with buggery when he was a teenager – not a happy experience. The discussion returned to conflict between men and the difficulty of facing it in such a group. I commented that although this was undoubtedly true it did not seem to prevent a high degree of ranking behaviour. The group knew to what this referred as it had been the subject of fairly exhaustive analysis in the past. The man who had earlier disclosed his difficulty in presenting himself positively in interviews commented that he was afraid of being attacked by other men if he was too positive in his self-presentation. I intervened to say that maybe this referred to men's difficulty in coping with envy of other men and other men's envy. There then followed a discussion about the homicidal nature of all competition, that the desire to kill is basic to it. Someone else pointed out that in primate conflicts this does not seem to be true, but that display is usually sufficient and that an unambiguous signal of submission will usually end violent conflict.

It is at times like this that I feel especially privileged. Of course I think as a group analyst. I am constantly alert to unconscious themes, to transferences between individuals and with the group and with me as the conductor. It is also at times like this that I believe one should take the group seriously and, insofar as one can, leave the manifest content alone. My first departure from the standard analytic goal – to make the unconscious conscious – is that this is not always or even mostly necessary in group treatment. Apart from the fact that to attempt to do so would be profoundly intrusive it would also render the group ineffective.

Competition, male rivalry or phallic display are endemic. Collectively, they are often referred to as 'spraying the testosterone' in my men's groups. Although such discussions are accompanied by humour in groups, it should not mislead us into thinking that the issues are less than critically serious for men. The consequences of losing such competition are potentially devastating. It is well known that one of the major motives for murder is the avoidance of shame or humiliation. This is testament to the underlying anxiety such encounters contain. Interestingly, in road rage incidents, which of course usually involve only men, over 95% of those where the drivers actually get out of their cars and challenge each other end without physical violence. In general they end with no loss of face to either after much threatening and display behaviour, rather like similar confrontations between animals.

There is an interesting aside to the notion of spraying the testosterone. It is commonly assumed that this hormone is responsible for men's aggression and for the lack of it by women. In other words, it is assumed to be gendered and biologically based. It has to be said that the experimental data is equivocal about this hypothesis.

A recent study at UCLA showed an interesting and important deviation from a biological deterministic position. Levels of aggression in a group of primates given extra testosterone increased markedly but the aggression was structured in the same way as prior to the administration of the extra testosterone. The troop members continued to act aggressively only towards lower ranked members. This provides a new dimension of understanding of aggression. Specifically, it shows that, although aggression may be mediated by testosterone, it is a learned set of behaviours. It is symbolically constructed and structured and it has meaning and intent rather than being random and unmotivated. This gives optimism to our attempts to find social and psychological solutions to problems of aggression and violence.

These considerations also speak to the men's rivalry and competition and the associated consequences of winning and losing. Does anyone need convincing of the intensity of men's need to compete and the desire to win and the fear of losing? The conclusion that competing is very intimately connected to constructions of masculinity, both socially and individually, surely is inescapable.

What does it mean to lose a competition with another man and what light might this shed on men's relationships with women? If all competition between men is unconsciously to the death and winning and losing are experienced as killing or being killed it is not surprising that so many men are deeply conflicted about competition. It is for this reason that many men are afraid of a challenge. Insofar as the place of women in this male drama is concerned, the first and obvious point is that any man who loses feels himself to be not as much of a man as his rival and therefore as being less fit to have the woman, who of course is simply an object of exchange in this male drama. This being 'less of a man' occasions anxiety and feelings of shame and humiliation. I cannot count the number of sessions I have listened to men recounting their feelings of rage at rivals who have defeated them. Its intensity is hard to believe. The situations are myriad, from being cut up on the road to losing at sport or, less transparently, a team one supports being defeated.

Biologists tell us that competitiveness serves evolutionary functions insofar as winners get to mate more often with equally superior opposite sex partners and that their superior strength or prowess in culturally valued activities will ensure that their offspring will be more likely to be successful and survive to produce offspring. Does losing therefore signify the loss of the opportunity to procreate with the female of choice? This could certainly occasion the feeling of not being as much of a man as one's conqueror. However, such feelings are not confined only to competition but also to situations involving loss of status or failure in general. I vividly recall my own feelings when I wanted to go into hiding after having been deferred for a year to begin training at my institute. I felt I should have a sign on my forehead announcing my failure and consequent lower status. I was able to work through those feelings but they were profoundly painful then and, no doubt, would be equally painful if a similar situation were to arise. Success and outward signs of it seem to be essential for self-esteem and attractiveness. This seems equally true whatever one's place in the social order although what the signifiers are must be different in different social contexts. The struggle for status is universal and one author has hypothesized it as a 'hunger' in a recent publication.[5] Recent research suggests that a majority of people would sacrifice some of their salary for a more prestigious job title even where it did not mean a change of duties. My clinical experience with women leads me to believe that such status struggles may be as common amongst women as they are amongst men although they lack the homicidal intensity.

Although I am not yet finished with the subject of phallic narcissism, at this point I wish to move to a different issue which arose in my work with phallic narcissistic wounds, whether being 'dissed', losing status or a competition etc. In the meantime I sincerely hope the reader is beginning to appreciate the significance of phallic narcissism to the construction of masculinity in what we might call 'averagely expectable conditions'. I now want to look more closely at its vicissitudes in the development of perversion.

10
Shame and Perversion

There is little doubt that shame – as distinct from associated states such as embarrassment, guilt or humiliation – is a major hurdle for most men in psychotherapy. I know this to be the case when the therapist is male, but I imagine it to be the case also with female therapists, where the dynamics are presumably different. Shame has its origins in the ego ideal and for men this is heavily invested with phallic narcissism. The ego ideal is that part of the superego which the ego (or self) aspires to emulate. It is the kind of person one aspires to be – the ideal self. As we have seen, in relation to masculinity this can amount to the imposition of demands to the point of persecution. This seems to be so particularly in relation to definitions of appropriate masculine behaviour with other men. Shame is an attachment-based emotion. It is learned in interaction with primary attachment figures. Nowhere is shame so apparent as in work with men who are sexually perverse. My definition of perversity is broader than you might imagine. I include in it the use of pornography for masturbation. Naturally, this rather enlarges the number of men who might be considered perverse and is quite different from the standard Freudian definition which assumes a normative sexuality which, however precarious, constitutes the outcome of normal sexual development. Freud regarded polymorphous perverse sexuality as the norm during early pre-Oedipal sexual development – in other words he saw perversion as a normal developmental way station with fixation, the failure to pass through it, leading to adult perversion. This he defines as a deviation from the normative outcome – sexual intercourse involving the aim of penetration and ejaculation into the vagina of a desired woman using only an erect penis. So the aim is clear as is the object. Perversion is when there is deviation from this normal outcome with respect to either aim or object. Perversion ignores the Oedipus complex with its structured sexuality so that perversions are constituted according to raw infantile sexual impulses and unresolved 'component instincts'. For example the object may be a shoe or other fetish such as rubber or fur, or be a body part – knee, foot or anus. The object may be incestuous (at one time we would have added homosexual to this) and the aim may be to look or exhibit or to cause pain or suffering as in sado-masochism, or to perform cunnilingus or fellatio or to urinate of defecate on the object. Actually, the range of aims and objects is myriad and sometimes it is hard to relate to the excitement that a perverse person can experience in relation to his chosen perversion.

Distinct from neuroses and psychoses, perversions imply the cessation of psychosexual development in a polymorphous pre-Oedipal stage. Since they are not based on the resolution of the Oedipus complex (whatever that may be, apart from this simple operational definition) and castration anxiety but on its denial, perversions are marked by the *refusal to acknowledge the f/actuality of sexual difference, i.e. the absence of a penis on women.*

It is hard to imagine any other form of presenting pathology which is so redolent with shame as sexual perversion. Actually there are times with perverse men when it is hard to understand why such intense shame should be attached to the behaviour in question. We normally think of shame as a socially based emotion, that it is based on our perceptions of how other people see us. However, this is often just so much projection. What is it then that is being projected? Fundamentally it is the idea that the other holds us in low esteem, has little or no respect for us. When ashamed, we are convinced that the other can see into us and discern both our shame and its causes (clearly a projection of one's feelings about oneself). Shame is a product of a relationship between our 'self' and an internal object or set of ideas which might be thought of as an internal object. In this case the object is the ideal self – the self one aspires to be or even, at times of grandiosity, believes one is. Let me illustrate.

Ken

Ken first presented to me as a very successful businessman. He was a partner in a very successful business and his job, involving transactions using millions of pounds, was very pressured. In his late 30s, he was a highly ranked black belt martial arts expert. His marriage, by which there were four children, was in serious difficulty. He and his wife had seen a marital therapist for two years to try to deal with what they jointly agreed was the cause of the difficulty but the therapist, a skilled experienced woman, was completely at a loss to understand his problem. This was that Ken, for all the signs of masculinity, was a secret transvestite and bondage fetishist. He was in fact hyper-masculine and this was in complete contradiction of the activity of his inner world and his private sexual life. Clearly his extreme masculinity was, amongst other things, a compensation for his private world. His sexual life was almost entirely perverse. He presented as charming and softly spoken and was a likeable man. It would have been impossible to know the private struggles with sexual shame he had suffered all his life and naturally it was very difficult for him to begin disclosing his secret life.

Although he and his wife had an active sexual relationship, he was rarely satisfied with it. His goal in sex was to give her as many orgasms as he could, mainly orally. He understood, quickly, that he was afraid he could not satisfy her with his penis and that he was actually masturbating inside her. He could achieve orgasm, usually, only by her articulating a fantasy of dressing him in her clothes, tying him up and performing fellatio on him. Otherwise he would fantasize this process until he ejaculated. On a regular basis he asked her to do this for him when the children were out of the house or they had specially arranged for this in order that he might do so in relative safety. She was required to tie him up so that he could not escape and she often did so and left the house with him tied up. This is the only time he felt safe and relaxed. Sometimes she would leave him for hours before returning to fellate him to orgasm and release him. A great source of tension arose from the fact that he always wanted her to 'give him a blow job' whilst he was still bound and she was very reluctant to do so, preferring instead to masturbate him. An even greater source of tension was her strengthening reluctance to get involved in his perversion at all. He was becoming increasingly resentful of her resistance and the marriage was disintegrating into chronic arguments. As I discovered, he was beginning to have affairs. This presented a real threat to his marriage (more so than it might for other men) as, in common with most perverts, he idealized his mistresses and invariably fantasized leaving his family for them.

His wife, Karen, whom I met once, was a stereotypical and highly feminine woman. She presented as quietly spoken, thoughtful and deeply concerned with Ken's welfare. She worried about his emotional fragility and his vulnerability to the depressions into which he frequently, and seriously, fell. In appearance she was hyper-feminine. Her make-up and hair were flawless. He informed me that she often took two hours to prepare herself for the day. She was also a fitness fanatic, dedicated to the point of obsession with attaining a 'perfect feminine' shape and preserving her youthful appearance. Perhaps it will come as a surprise to hear that her preferred sexual position was on top of him. By his account she loved to dominate him. When I suggested to him that she was a phallic woman, this normally concrete man had no difficulty with this complex image, which is not surprising when we consider that this complex object is at the core of his perversion.

For the first two years of his once-weekly treatment (inadequate I know, but unavoidable given the distances from his home to London) his sessions mainly concerned his cross-dressing and bondage activities and what came to be known as his anti-depressants – his mistresses. His shame was a major issue and, at times, in a rather contradictory way as we shall see. His bondage/cross-dressing episodes would usually begin with a period of intense fantasizing. He struggled intensely with his compulsion to act out his guilty, shame-laden fantasy. The dissonance, and the gap, between his public and private selves were immense. The fantasy was always present, though not always intrusively so. It became clear that it only became intrusive and compelling when he suffered a reverse in his life or when he had been subjected to what he experienced as a humiliation or shaming by Karen in particular but also from anyone else. It was not always possible to understand the reverse from his material as he was much given to denial of his vulnerabilities. Often it would take much patient unpacking of his associations for an apparently irrelevant detail to assume its full significance. A typical session early in his treatment shaped the way we were to eventually understand his perversion.

He reported that the fantasy was very strong and he believed that he would have to act it out once he arrived home. He had almost casually remarked that a few days ago he had passed, in the street, one of his former partners from a failed business venture of some years ago and that this encounter had 'upset' him (this lack of emotional differentiation is common in perversion). From there he talked about problems at work, his day-to-day difficulties with his present partners, none of them particularly pressing. His associations then drifted to his anticipated conflict with Karen when he asked for a 'session'. He thought she now used every request for a 'session' to humiliate and shame him about his perverse sexuality. All this was quite familiar by now and in the slight lull which followed I asked him a quite innocent question about his former partner, not in any expectation of eliciting anything of substance but more to relieve my developing fatigue (a common reaction of mine in working with perversion). He told me that the business failure had been engineered by this man and that he had arranged it so that Ken would end up with legal responsibility for the company's debts. As Ken was relating this story he became increasingly agitated and his language descended into obscenity. When he saw the former partner in the street he had wanted to kill him. That he possessed the skills to do so was not in doubt. However, he talked about his fears that if he did mount an attack he might come off the worse for it. He asked me whether I thought he lacked 'bottle'. He knew that walking away was the right thing to have done but worried that he was just making excuses for his cowardice. I made the point that so long as he was afraid he could never know if he had bottled when he did what he knew to be the right thing and that no amount of reassurance would be of value as he felt so shamed by his fear. He went on to describe the intensity of his feelings of having been humiliated and the shame at having let his partner get away with it because of his fear of further humiliation and shame should he lose that fight. He felt an overpowering sense of injustice as he described how his former partner had taken him for a ride. He spent a couple of hours after seeing him in a fantasy of the things he might have done at the time. Mostly these consisted of inflicting serious physical harm on the man and emerging victorious with his honour satisfied and his self-respect regained. A lot of this is fairly standard grist for the analytic mill but it also raises more questions than it answers. Let us look at the obvious connections first. He feels castrated by this man. He feels impotent to redress the injustice. He fears that if he attacks he will be beaten and even more seriously damaged. This can all be worked through from a standard Oedipal perspective much of which will emerge inevitably in the transference – presuming the therapist wants to go there. The more interesting questions concern the connections between this material and his bondage and transvestism. Why should any of this lead to such an intense fantasy and with such perverse content? The standard Oedipal process in such situations would involve fantasy of victorious attack, feelings of shame for not having had the courage to mount such an attack and a combination of gradual working through and suppression of these feelings until internal equanimity and some measure of self-respect or esteem was restored. This could lead eventually to some sort of reality-based modification in the ego ideal and an acceptance of one's ordinary human and male limitations. In analysis the castration anxieties would need to be kept in consciousness more directly and the repression or suppression interpreted. It seemed fairly clear to both Ken and I that it was this encounter with his former partner, which had led directly to his intense fantasy and his need for a 'session' as he called his cross-dressing episodes. The significance of the word was not lost on me.

Ken's background was as troubled as you might imagine. He had been raised by a very neurotic mother and an alcoholic father. His mother had conducted a long term affair with the lodger in the family home since Ken was a baby. Ken's father periodically moved out because he found this very hard to cope with once it was discovered. It seems he had effectively capitulated without any significant protest. The mother had eventually become pregnant by the lodger and effectively set up home with him and evicted her husband. Ken had stayed with the mother except for one short period when he had been very happy to be with his father but very unhappy with his local school. This had led to his returning to his mother's home and his new stepfather. Ken is one of the very few patients I have worked with who has spontaneously recovered memories of sexual abuse. Initially he remembered his stepfather squeezing his genitals so hard that he cried in pain. This was accompanied by intense feelings of humiliation, anger and grief. Later, as a result of a dream of being seduced from which he woke in a panic, he had gradually remembered being sexually abused by his seven years older sister from age seven to nine. She had forced him to engage in mutual masturbation and on many occasions to penetrate her as she sat on top of him (note, Karen's favourite position). This ceased abruptly when she left the home to marry at the age of 16. None of these memories was associated with pleasure, only great anxiety.

In fact, his recovery of these memories led to a difficult period for us both. His anxiety and his grief overwhelmed him and at times he became depressed and quite suicidal. There were times when I feared he might carry out his oft-repeated plan to walk into an Underground train. His cross-dressing became very important during this period, often seeming to be his only defence against even more serious breakdown. It is interesting that his fragmented 'perverse' self was his strongest defence against a major breakdown. This is very important for our understanding of perversion as a denial of sexual difference and support for Freud's conclusion that perversion is the 'negative of neurosis'. My disagreement with that is a product of our 21st century understanding of emotional disorder compared with his 19th century psychiatric taxonomy. My experience is that perversion is a defence against serious mental distress, depression being the most obvious.

Attachment

It had become clear to me early in his treatment that Ken's attachment style was disorganized/chaotic/unresolved (see Chapter 2). He frequently described how he felt frozen when there was any hint of reproach in Karen's voice. He experienced a state of inner collapse, not unlike the state often described by victims of bullying. This is the state that Main calls 'fright without solution'.[1] It occurs when the infant has simultaneous impulses to both approach and to flee from the caregiver, what conditioning theorists call 'approach-avoidance conflict'. This occurs when the source of the anxiety which initiates the attachment system (fundamentally the need to be close to the attachment figure for protection) is also the source of the relief from the anxiety. Frequent experiences of such treatment will lead to the development of disorganized attachment. In conditions of stress in adulthood when the attachment system is activated, there will be a breakdown of the behavioural strategies required to relieve the stress, paradigmatically equal to the breakdown in infancy when faced with a primary carer who was frightening. Individuals who as infants developed disorganized attachment will frequently as adults become very controlling in attachments.[2] Ken frequently described how Karen's mother had constantly shamed and humiliated her father and reduced him to a 'shadow of a man'. Karen's treatment of Ken was so similar to her mother's treatment of her father, and his own mother's treatment of his father, as to be indistinguishable. He recounted how she had effectively taken a poll of her friends – most of whom were known to Ken – as to their feelings about his need to cross-dress and be bound. He cringed with shame when he talked about this. She also frequently reduced him to tears with her remorseless attacks on him about his masculinity, or lack of it. She accused him of being homosexual or of being unfaithful with other women (which was true, but nowhere near so often as the accusations). The fact is that he lived in an atmosphere of fairly constant emasculation, experientially if not actually. The stronger the attack the more likely it would lead to an activation of his cross-dressing and bondage fantasy and the need to act it out. This raises the question I asked earlier: Why should any of this lead to such a perversion?

There is another very relevant piece of information concerning the origins of the fantasy. When he was eight years old, and during his sister's abuse of him, Ken had seen a film called *Von Ryan's Express*. In this, an actress, was bound and gagged on the train. Ken had found these scenes very exciting though in a physically undifferentiated way. He was quite clear that it was not genitally arousing. He believes he did not experience erection until he was 12 or 13 although this was clearly a false memory designed to enable his denial of his sister's rape of him. How was he able to penetrate his sister – something of which he was equally certain? However, he had a vivid memory of saying to himself 'I'll have some of that' as he watched these scenes. It is an equally important question as to why 'having some of that' should eventually mean identifying with her and being tied up, rather than tying up and dominating and humiliating women. Not that he was completely uninterested in being top dog. He was interested in bondage/cross-dressing pornography and enjoyed tying Karen up. You can see at first sight that one radically different element in being top dog with a woman is that a woman cannot cross-dress as a woman. 'Being a woman', as in 'castrated', is central to Ken's fantasy structure although he clearly sees women as phallic. As a matter of some interest, although Karen mildly enjoyed being tied up and beaten whilst dressed in her most feminine underwear, this was not an element in Ken's drama or fantasy. Although he would beat her he did not enjoy doing so. This may seem odd considering that his determination to demonstrate his masculinity is only equalled by his terror that he will fail in the attempt.

Stoller makes the point that all transvestites have had the experience of being cross-dressed as children by women (for a child all women are powerful) and that this will not always be consciously recalled.[3] I have worked in depth with quite a large number of transvestites (who it must be said are not all the same[4]) and in not one of them did we discover a history of having been cross-dressed although they had all dressed in their mother's or carer's clothes as children and young boys. Where my findings do agree with Stoller's is in the fact that all my patients had, or recovered, memories of feeling deeply humiliated and shamed by women in childhood and that this was also a major factor in their adult lives. This shaming or humiliating experience could be having been rejected or abandoned by their mother, which of course implies the most shameful of all secrets – that one is not lovable. That Ken felt shamed and humiliated by his sister's abuse was beyond doubt. And what of his mother? He had very little memory of her until about the age when the incestuous abuse began. His adult relation with her was enough to serve as a guide to her behaviour in his early life. He described her as 'fucking crazy', 'unbearable', interfering', 'incapable of listening', 'insensitive'. All in all he could hardly bear to be in her company and would go to great lengths to avoid her. We began to gradually piece together memories of his early latency and his memories of his mother were the childhood equivalent of his adult perceptions. It was not hard to imagine the conflict he felt. On the one hand he needed her as any child would need his mother and on the other she was the source of intense anxiety for him. He vividly recalled her coldness to him and how she would not touch or cuddle him when he was small. This surely was the origin of his disorganized attachment and of many of his difficulties with Karen.

However, there are many men in the world who would describe their mothers in similar terms and whilst being disturbed would still never dream of cross-dressing and bondage. At this point it may help to say that women obviously know something about men and female clothes that maybe most men would deny. It is that a very large number of normal men have more than a passing interest in women's lingerie and, more importantly, what it hides – the fantasy that something is hidden. So is it possible that there is a connection between men's normal interest in women's lingerie and Ken's and others' cross-dressing? It was widely publicized that David Beckham, a well-known English sportsman, regularly dressed in his wife's underwear when he went out. It was said that it helped this, reputedly quite shy, anxious man to feel secure. Presumably he felt that he was taking with him a little of her – that in some way her underwear had become a transitional object connecting him with her. But why wear it? Why not carry it in a pocket or some other place of concealment? Of course it may be simply convenient to wear her underwear rather than carry it, but I believe the motivation is more complex than this. It seems obvious that at some level he is putting himself inside her skin – at least her second skin – and that his fantasy, and the security deriving from it, is that in some way he is inside her and being protected by her. This is rather an interesting speculation because it would certainly go some way to explaining at least part of what Ken is up to when he cross-dresses and it would take it out of the encapsulated world of perverse narcissism and back to the world of attachment objects and relationships with them (another crucial part of what it does is provide the lingerie with what it so obviously lacks – a penis). I believe that this step is crucial to help us understand what it is that Ken himself is trying to reach. It must also be remembered that he was most compelled to dress in Karen's clothes when he felt humiliated and shamed by her or when she questioned his masculinity. Dressing in women's clothes makes him feel safe – he never felt safer than when dressed as a woman. Interestingly, it took some time to discover what will now be obvious, that the first feminine clothes in which Ken had cross-dressed were, in fact, his mother's, and there had been at least one occasion when she had seen him masturbating whilst doing so and had pretended not to notice.

What of the bondage? As we gradually unpacked his fantasy structure, which to this point had taken about three years, it was becoming clear that Ken suffered from paralysing shame about his masculinity, or what he considered his lack of it. He remembered an incident in Thailand when he had gone there on a business trip and, with colleagues, had visited a brothel. When he had undressed in the woman's room she had begun laughing 'hysterically' (his words) and pointing at his penis, saying 'tiny cock'. He had been reduced to tears of shame. Needless to say, he did not attempt to have sex with her. When I questioned him about this reaction, the absence of anything resembling anger was astonishing. In fact this was typical of his response when a woman treated him badly. He would be devastated with feelings of helplessness, passivity and depression, sometimes suicidal – but angry feelings were entirely absent. As we unpacked his statement that he never felt so 'safe and relaxed' as when he was bound, it became clear that he not only felt 'held and contained' but that he knew he could not be a danger to anyone. The need to feel held and contained (which he never otherwise felt) was the driving force beneath his perversion. Fundamentally it was a defence against a profound suicidal depression (experienced when he recovered the memory of his sister's rape of him).

At this point in his treatment his self-esteem had improved markedly. He was at a stage where he was able to respond to his wife's attacks with self-assertion and appropriate boundary setting. In fact, after a while, when it was clear that she was unable to change her behaviour in this regard, he left her and began divorce proceedings. It had become increasingly clear to him that his cross-dressing and bondage activity was the glue that held them together and as our work gradually reduced his shame and the compulsion to act out, at least with her, she had become more aggressive to him in what was seemingly an attempt to get him to plead for a 'session', an activity which she said she hated.

It was at about this point that Ken's guilt became a central focus of our work and something, which should have been blindingly obvious from the outset, made itself known to us. We had grown so used to unpacking the cross-dressing that the bondage element of his perversion had faded into the background. We had frequently returned to it, but only briefly as it defied any attempts on his part to think beyond the concrete reality of it. Concrete thinking is par for 'perverts' (one might as well add, for most men). This is one reason why the work with perversion can be so slow and, at times, boringly repetitive.

During a discussion of his sister's abuse of him he had mentioned that he had the memory of something covering his face. He had the feeling of something being done to him against his will, of being forced. He associated this to his fear of his penis being hurt whenever he penetrated a woman. This was such that he always spit into his hand to lubricate her vagina and prevent any painful friction. I said something to the effect that sex was always associated with pain and guilt. At that moment I realized the obvious. Every orgasm he had was associated with being forced or, effectively, raped. He was unable to orgasm during intercourse without the fantasy of bondage and usually reached it at the moment when he was tied up in fantasy. In his cross-dressing/bondage activity he was made to orgasm by being fellated or masturbated while he was still tied. He never actually did it to himself or, on the few occasions when this had been necessary, it had been 'not worth doing it'. Contrary to his first sexual experiences (and as a defence against the overwhelming anxiety they caused) he had constructed a woman's sexuality as passive (tied and bound). She is forced to have sex. He identified clearly with this feminine construction in his perversion but in the end he triumphed over the phallic woman (his sister) by demonstrating his phallic potency as he ejaculated. He further demonstrated it by subsequently bringing his partner to repeated orgasm through cunnilingus.

It was during this period when I recognized something else which should have been blindingly obvious – the possibility that Ken had been swaddled as a baby. A quick check with his mother confirmed that this was so.

In early discussions about his adolescent masturbatory activity he had always maintained that he could not and did not masturbate at all during his teens. Now, however, a different story emerged. He recalled his first orgasm had occurred when he had dressed in his mother's tights and loosely bound his hands. He had an erection and had begun pushing himself into the floor until he eventually had an orgasm. He had gone into a real panic attack, fearing and believing he had done himself some damage (transparently an attack of guilt of obvious origins). However, he repeated this process and it soon became the only way he could reach orgasm. The point is that he was not masturbating even though he was having orgasms. When he was bound he was not responsible for his orgasm and therefore did not have to feel guilty about his sexuality and its incestuous roots. In fact he was only capable of orgasm when bound or fantasizing he was bound. Let us return to the two questions of most interest. What did it mean that he cross-dressed and could only orgasm with this present or in fantasy, and why does he need to be tied up and fellated or masturbated by his wife? I believe I have answered these questions and the process as it is written is very much the process we followed in analysing Ken's perversion and finally dissolving any shame and guilt about his sexuality. It is important to say that his perversion never disappeared – in fact they never do, in my experience, although they undergo substantial modification. Although at the outset his goal was to 'get rid of' his perversion it became clear that this would be impossible and his goal evolved into something altogether different and satisfying for him.

He was faced with a number of critical dilemmas and conflicts during his development and his perversion was specifically evolved to contain and manage these. As I see them, and as we developed our understanding, they were:

- How to prevent fragmentation, suicidal despair and depression.
- How to metabolize the trauma of his sister's abuse of him.
- How to manage his deep feelings of castration and impotence – potentiated by the strong identification with the emasculated father.
- How to become sexual whilst experiencing the most intense feelings of guilt and shame, not only about his abuse, but also his incestuous desires for his mother and his subsequent castration anxieties related to his stepfather. Not forgetting that his incestuous desires were fused with profound and guilt laden rage towards his mother and his sister.
- His terror of intimacy with a woman and his profound regressive need for protection and safety in an attachment.

I hope you can see how his sexual activity enabled him to convert these traumas into triumphs. Effectively, his orgasm asserted the triumph of his phallic masculinity in the face of each of these. Of course the cost was high in that he was incapable of genuine intimacy with a woman – the terror of which is shared by all cross-dressers.

Finally I want to address the end of Ken's treatment, which lasted for nine years. The patient working through of his sexuality led to a dissolution of his shame and guilt about his 'perverse' behaviour. More importantly it un-coupled it from the need to feel shamed and humiliated in order to experience his sexuality and enabled him to make it part of a consensual relationship not based on his need to constantly defend against emasculation. He arrived at a point where in his search for a partner he was able to be completely transparent about his sexuality before becoming deeply involved with anyone and he finally found a relationship with a woman whose interests dovetailed almost perfectly with his.

I hope I have not given the impression that this was all achieved with a nice bow tied around it and without loose ends. Far from it. There are many unanswered questions which would repay thoughtful analysis. However, the struggle to understand, the patient attention and manifest confusion all contributed to what both Ken and I regard as a successful conclusion. Many of the benefits were reached simply by the commitment to the process and by those elements of it which fall outside the control of either participant.

To conclude, I arrived at the point where I re-assessed all the work I was doing with cross-dressers and concluded that it is effectively impossible for a cross-dressing man to live with a woman who is not supportive of his sexuality and unwilling to be actively involved with it. I have also concluded that it is rare for any cross-dresser to face the intensity of the rage and hatred he has towards women and which is so clear in the material. I have worked with many and only one did so – he gave up relationships.

11
Normal Hyper-masculinity

In my work with violent and perverse men over the last 30 years I have reached the conclusion that a straightforwardly psychodynamic approach is doomed to failure if it has as its objective to stop the behaviour although it may be very successful if its aims are simply analysis and understanding.

When I first began to work with what I initially thought of as deviant men I did so from an orthodox frame of reference. Orthodoxy in this context means that I believed the behaviour, whether violence, emotional and psychological abuse or perversion, to be symptomatic of underlying difficulties. This is the standard psychodynamic model in which the triangle of conflict[1] contains an underlying impulse, which generates anxiety and then defence or resistance. Violence towards or abuse of others is considered to be a result of having been abused and then through a complex defensive known as identification with the aggressor the victim becomes a perpetrator in order to master the trauma.

The analytic task is to firstly interpret the resistance or defence with reference to the underlying anxiety and then, at an appropriate time, to interpret the relation of the anxiety to the underlying impulse. In this model, the 'deviant', violent or abusive behaviour is seen as contingent on the underlying anxiety and impulse and could not be expected to remit until these had been made conscious and worked through in the transference. There are many reasons why this model is flawed when working with men who are disturbing rather than disturbed. Perhaps one of the most important is that there is simply no evidence that insight into the unconscious leads to behavioural change. This is rather galling for all of us who struggle daily to make the unconscious conscious. However, there is relief in knowing that many of our patients do not want behavioural change but simply to feel better. There is for me a more important reason why this model is flawed. It is that whilst the therapist and patient struggle with this task (and I want to make it clear that I do regard it as essential) there is somewhere a victim, or victims, of this man's behaviour who is possibly at risk of death or, in the case of children, long term damage to their emotional and mental health. In my view it is unacceptable to regard this as inevitable until the underlying pathology has been mitigated or resolved. This is particularly so when there are available models and techniques of treatment which we now know can be effective in changing behaviour within weeks and months rather than years. It is worth re-iterating that although I have spent much time describing abusive men, I regard the differences between them and non-abusers as quantitative. In my view, all men suffer the 'domino' syndrome described earlier (see Chapter 6) and we know that 40% of men will acknowledge having hit a partner at some time in their life. I do not think it is stretching imagination to suppose that the proportion of men who are controlling and emotionally abusive is very much higher.

My complacent acceptance of the orthodoxy with violent abusers was rather rudely shattered by a developing acquaintance with Sandra Horley of what was, at that time, Chiswick women's Aid (now known as Refuge). She pointed out some rather obvious facts by asking simple questions:

- If men's abuse of women is determined by insecurity or underlying trauma of whatever sort why is it that women with underlying insecurities or traumatic childhoods do not abuse men or, so far as we know, anyone else?[2]

- Given we know the abuse of women and girl children is endemic and the perpetrators are overwhelmingly male should we not expect many more women to be perpetrators if a history of being abused is the cause of becoming an abuser?
- If being controlling and/or abusive is an illness or a sickness, which the orthodox treatment model implies, how can it be that so many men are sick? Although accurate figures are difficult to come by given the methodological differences in incidence studies, it is certain that somewhere between 10 and 20% of men have physically abused their female partner and that 10% do so frequently and with great intensity. When questioned closely, most women will acknowledge that their male partners attempt to control them and 40% of men will disclose an incident of partner abuse.
- If being violent to a woman is symptomatic of loss of control as a diagnosis of impulse control disorder would imply, why is it that men usually only abuse their wives or girlfriends and not strangers?
- If alcohol causes violence why do men not hit people in the pub rather than waiting till they get home to be violent? Why does the bottle have the woman's name on it? Why is he not violent every time he drinks?

The questions go on and on. In fact it is embarrassingly easy to undo orthodox explanations of men's violence to women. All we are required to do is ask whether women who share the hypothesized cause of violent and abusive behaviour by men are in fact violent and abusive. The simple answer in our present state of knowledge is *no*. There seems not to be a factor shared by men and women and which men and professionals offer as causal explanation, which makes women violent and abusive. Ultimately we are left with the only thing that abusive men have in common and do not share with women – they are male.

Theoretically, things start to get really interesting at this point. If the only factor shared by most abusers is their masculinity can we then say that their violence is caused by it? In that case do we then end up defining masculinity as a form of pathology? This is not so far fetched as it sounds. I want to further this study of masculinity by looking at a certain form of pathological masculinity to see if it can help us understand the 'normal' masculinity this book is about. This formally defined masculinity is manifestly more disturbing than disturbed. At its most extreme it might be called sociopathy (in past times it was referred to as psychopathy) or, less frighteningly, anti-social personality disorder.

These days we do not talk much about psychopathy, rather the discourse is centred on the Anti-Social Personality Disorder which is characterized by a consistent disregard for the rights and feelings of others and for the basic laws of society. Characteristics of ASPD include deceitfulness, impulsivity, irresponsibility, irritability and lack of remorse. Most, if not all of these qualities or traits seem to be empirically associated with failed attachment during infancy and in particular with the development of a dismissive attachment style and states of mind. When we look closely at these qualities or traits of personality we may be surprised that many of them are quite ordinary in many of the men we know personally, including those we are closest to. However, one should state the obvious that anyone possessing many of these traits or even a few in extreme degree would find it hard to live a healthy and fulfilling life. Even more surprising is the fact that many of the most successful men we can think of also possess many of these qualities, even if not in marked degree. In fact it is obvious that many are rewarded greatly in certain fields of activity, such as business or warfare. This is not to say that such qualities are necessary for success, but it may be that they make success more likely under certain circumstances. In fact, not only are men more likely to be diagnosed as anti-social personalities, up to seven times more likely, but some research,

and my extensive clinical experience, shows that a dismissive
or detached attachment style, perhaps the most important trait
of ASPs, seems to be normal for men. I have worked with over
1,000 men in the last 40 years and the majority of them have
a great many of the qualities required for an ASP diagnosis,
although not in excessive degree or the degree required for such a
diagnosis. The differences are quantitative not qualitative. What
is quite patently obvious is that the most violent of these men,
including those whom I have met in secure institutions, have
been severely damaged in childhood or infancy or both. I have
come to view ASP as a response and defence against the pain of
trauma. The easiest way to defend against further trauma from
others is simply to denigrate them so that one need never have a
meaningful relationship with anyone. In extremis, they can be so
denigrated that one can in addition, physically damage them with
impunity simply because they are less than human and become
simply objects. However, it is not my intention here to investigate
ASP. Rather my intention is to see what, if anything, we might
learn about masculinity from looking at this apparently uniquely
hyper-masculine profile of ASP. Of particular interest is how this
might help us in our attempts to deal with what Jim Gilligan calls
the epidemic of our time, violence.[3] I will attempt to illustrate
with a detailed history of a man who in his earlier life might
have fulfilled the conditions for this diagnosis but who, when
he came to me, was more simply hyper-masculine. However, he
had undergone some significant changes before he came to me
and which I believe led to a more optimistic prognosis than is
usually the case and in fact led to a good outcome.

Ronald is a highly intelligent man of 35 who has a history
of extreme alcohol and drug abuse. Much of this was syntonic
in the industry in which he worked. He had realized he had a
serious problem when he had been on the verge of substantial
success, involving the fulfilment of a childhood wish and a real
fortune, and he had gone out of his way to actively destroy

his opportunity. Lest anyone misunderstand me let me say that I do not measure a person's value as being coterminous with what they are worth, by the amount of money they own. Nor do I regard money as a measure of success except in the crudest possible way. I cannot count the number of rich men I have worked with who were deeply unhappy and would have swapped a large measure of their fortune for peace of mind or contentment (Freud said that the only things that could make anyone happy were the things desired in childhood and no child had ever wanted to be rich with money). Thereafter, Ronald had engaged in actively self-destructive behaviour involving drugs and alcohol in great quantities. Fortunately, he had survived all his efforts to destroy himself and had finally ended up in AA. This had undoubtedly saved his life. After a number of years of doing the basic, which is simply turning up to meetings, he was living with constant and extreme anxiety in his recovered state. He had realized that sobriety was only the first step and entered psychotherapy to get help with his fear. (Woody Allen says that life is 70% turning up. I would add that the other 30% is turning up on time.)

It was clear from our first meeting that Ronald was an extremely self-righteous angry man. He seemed to be under enormous internal pressure. It took many months for his story to emerge but from the first he poured out with great intensity an obsession that had been driving him for some time. He had been told when he was three years old that he was adopted and he had only recently – as the result of the birth of his first child (a very complex story here) – engaged in the search for his birth mother and family. His present relationship was in a state of virtually complete collapse. It did not take long to understand what had been happening. His adoptive mother had informed him of his status shortly after she became pregnant – something of which she had thought herself incapable. He remembered the profound sense of shock he had felt and how she seemed to have changed towards him from that moment on. After the birth of his stepbrother his mother had effectively ignored him. Ronald was unable to articulate the sense of injustice and pain he had felt ever since. What we both saw immediately (and which surprisingly he had never seen before) was that he had been, systematically, emotionally maltreating his partner, whom he had met in the fellowship, since she became pregnant. After the pregnancy his maltreatment of her escalated. He believed she had stopped loving him, because she did not want sex with him. He experienced her as rejecting, cold and dismissive. He believed she was over-involved with their son and that it was an unhealthy relationship (a clear example of first child syndrome and maternal transference). The exactness with which he had systematically recreated his experience during his adoptive mother's pregnancy and his position in the family as he experienced it after the birth was quite remarkable. He recalled his subsequent sulk in great detail. He described how pictures of him taken after the birth of his adoptive brother show him with an unhappy, glum, reluctant face. It was clear that he had been sulking ever since and that it had intensified when his present partner became pregnant and after the birth of their son. His sense of injustice was overwhelming at times. No amount of rational reasoning or reality testing could have any impact on him as he began to inflate himself into a state of righteous anger and homicidal rage. He would articulate the most violent fantasies during his times with me. He would talk of his desire to kill his birth mother and sister (whom he had managed to trace) with an intensity which bordered on the obsessive. He had discovered that he had been with his birth mother for six weeks before he was separated from her. He railed against her and his sister for their stupidity. Anyone who did not see the world as he did was inevitably stupid. He was possessed of the most hybristic personality I had ever encountered outside a secure institution. Initially I experienced states of fear of what violence he might do to me if I insisted he stop his self-inflation. I would have fantasies of appearing in court giving evidence in a case against him for multiple murder. After a while, however, I began to see that he actually represented very little physical risk to anyone, including me. His ventilating of his violent fantasies was a way of defusing them. I had little doubt also that my initial fears of and for him were his projected way of letting me know just how afraid and helpless he felt himself to be, both now in his relationship with his partner and as a child with his rejecting mother. The vulnerable and frightened parts of him were entirely split off and forcibly projected into any container (projective identification). It was not enough that he project these parts of himself – he had to see them being identified with. He could be truly disturbing.

It required very little empathy on my part to understand how Ronald might have felt as a young boy and how his early experience had shaped his subsequent life. It was also clear to me that the therapeutic task was to help him re-join the human race, from which in some real way he had effectively excluded himself since the birth of his adoptive brother.

This was no easy task. Like all very angry people he was deeply hurt and so much shame was attached to his neediness that the prospects of helping him to grieve seemed slim. Shortly after he began his treatment with me it became clear to us both that stopping his sulk was going to be very difficult. With the best will in the world he found it almost impossible to stop attributing malice or hostile intent to his partner, or indeed to anyone, and then retaliating. He had certainly reduced the intensity and frequency with which he did this, but we were both concerned that he had begun to project his vulnerable and frightened self into his son and blame his partner for the suffering he believed the child was enduring. That he had changed to some extent was evident from the fact that at this point his partner suggested they should separate. Previously she had been too afraid to make such a suggestion. What had become obvious to me soon after beginning with him was that during the early phases of his treatment normal interpretations would have very little effect on him. By 'normal' I mean interpretations which meet Malan's criteria[4] – firstly in the unpacking of 'the triangle of conflict' where the defence, the anxiety and the underlying impulse are all made clear and secondly in the context of the 'triangle of person' in which the connections between the three relationships, with the therapist (the transference), the person the patient is talking about and the original figure, usually the parent, are all understood (see Figure 11.1).

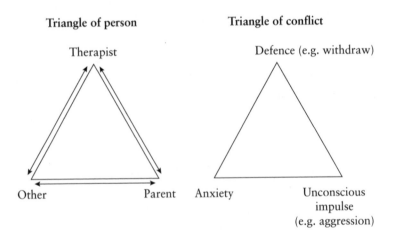

Figure 11.1   Triangles of person and conflict

Source: D. Malan. *Individual Psychotherapy and the Science of Psychodynamics.* 1978. Hodder Arnold.

In fact what I discovered with Ronald has a more general application to work with men. It is that a lot of men require a great deal of character analysis – a rather old fashioned term for an old fashioned activity. In my case it means the extensive use of the counter-transference and a greater willingness to get involved by articulating here and now experience. Felicity de Zulueta has expressed her conviction that analytic opacity, emotional distance and vocal neutrality are experienced as rejecting and frightening by people who have been abused and developed an insecure attachment style.[5] They simply do not feel held or contained by therapists who are comfortable behaving in this way. I could not agree more. The necessity to obviate this can clearly work against the analytic process. However, it does not work contrary to the therapeutic process. Valerie Sinason told me that when she applied to train as a psychoanalyst she heard it said that she had spent too much time working with abused, damaged and traumatized patients to ever become a psychoanalyst. Fortunately for her this turned out to be mistaken. Part of her genius is her willingness to involve herself with her patients. So what does involvement mean to me? First and foremost it means being much more transparent to my patients. This is not indiscriminate. I do not disclose any information about my private life or circumstances. However, I do say quite a lot about what is going on in my internal world after reflecting on it. I am also prepared to give frank descriptions of my patient's behaviour. I have told more than one that they are behaving obnoxiously – often to their great relief!

What is clear from Ronald is the connection between his deeply traumatized state (and many of his memories, in the form of bodily states, can only have come from his first six weeks in hospital after his birth) and his phallic narcissistic hyper-masculinity. The solution to the profound narcissistic wounds was to develop an equally profound phallic narcissistic personality and masculinity involving detachment, invulnerability, self-inflation, dismissiveness, contempt (as a defence against envy), premature independence, a threatening self-presentation, contempt for authority, etc. etc. Clearly the key to his treatment was to enable him to access his vulnerability and fear. This was achieved entirely by focusing on his reactions to breaks in treatment to the point where it was apparent to him that he had formed an attachment to me the loss of which was very frightening. There were occasions when he stood over me and screamed and threatened; there were others when he would impulsively head for the door telling me he would take no 'more of this shit'. Not pleasant or for the *too* faint hearted but ultimately rewarding as he discovered he could rely on me not to abandon him or reject him.

I want to stress that although there are many similarities between hyper-masculine men and normal men, these are qualitative. The real and crucial difference is that hyper-masculine men cross the line between thinking, feeling and action. Men who are closer to the mean do not cross that line – they may have the thinking and the feeling but there is a crucial difference which sets a limit to the behaviour. In my opinion that limit is set by the experience of having had some satisfying attachment in early life and not having been actively abused or traumatized as was the case in Ronald's history. There had been many times in his young adulthood when he had crossed that line. As he was fond of saying, 'I didn't deal with solicitors letters'. At times is was difficult to contain my anxiety when he was making threats against particular people; threats which I knew him to have carried out when he was younger.

His aggressive, anti-social and threatening behaviour was always occasioned by what he felt were threats or challenges to his potency – a potency which was entirely illusory and which in reflective moments he was able to acknowledge as such. Unfortunately, it is the case that people can be frightened into compliance and obedience and this was a lesson which he was never able to unlearn. He would frequently describe how there were two sets of rules, the one of the streets and the one in which people like psychotherapists live (yes, I was aware of the threat).

What was clear is that his hyper-masculinity was simply a more extreme version of the normal big M, normal phallic narcissistic masculinity. I also saw with great clarity the underlying grief and his unresolved terrors of loss and separation and the yearning for a secure attachment – an attachment he was able to develop with me as he worked through his separation anxieties. The correct handling of breaks in treatment, between session, at weekends and longer holiday breaks, was the key to this development and to the gradual mitigation of his hyper-masculinity and self-inflation. This is the crucial issue in helping hyper-masculine men and in helping those with insecure dismissive attachment. I also learned from Ronald that masculinity always refers to the big M, whether it is emasculated or hyper. In the end men calibrate their activities with the big M as the standard to be aspired to – averagely expectable phallic-narcissistic masculinity.

12
The Function of Drama

Freud was frustrated and perplexed by the problem of passivity and placed himself in all manner of theoretically difficult positions in his attempt to explain its contradictions. Basically, passivity is a problem with doing things. I can recall vividly my own analysis with David Malan when I, and he, suffered greatly with a complete unwillingness on my part actually to do anything. Most of the time I felt as though there was nothing I wanted to do but, interestingly, I did not feel at all depressed. His consistent content interpretation was that I was struggling with a conflict between doing things for myself and my unwillingness to do things for my parents, in particular my mother, because she had given me so little that I did not feel I had enough internal resources to spare to devote to doing other things. A subsidiary interpretation concerned my sulking and going on strike to punish her by withholding as she had withheld from me. Of course the process interpretations of the transference and counter-transference were the most important by far. Why did I want him to fail and feel frustrated even if it meant the possible failure of my analysis? Could it be that I was as angry with him as with my mother and wanted him to experience the frustration I had been made to feel as a child? Was I sulking with him? In his normal way, he presented these interpretations as questions rather than as certainties and encountered all the resistance you would expect from someone in such a state of mind. Incidentally, I have never held to the view that the transference should always be made explicit. If an interpretation is made about any relationship I believe it is always understood unconsciously that the same is being said about the analytic or therapeutic relationship. As far as possible I try to limit my explicit transference interpretations to those occasions when the transference is clearly functioning in the service of, or as a resistance.

Developmentally I have come to see passivity as being concerned with a child's initial conflicts with mobility, whether to crawl or walk and also with anally derived conflicts about giving and taking – demands – originating in the experience of maternal demands for toilet training. Fundamentally I believe the child feels he has not been given enough to have sufficient left over to gift to his mother. Clearly there are serious attachment difficulties here and one sees them repeated in the transference.

Passivity is highly conflicted for men. Doing nothing is the antithesis of masculinity which is primarily defined by activity or doing. As I have already said, masculinity is what men do – it is not some essential internal state which is easily differentiated from femininity. This is why external markers are so essential in defining and managing the 'essential' difference – the presence or absence of penis and breasts. Passivity is associated with femininity and unconsciously with castration. In the construction made famous by Freud, passivity is associated with masochism and femininity and activity is associated with sadism and masculinity. It is a cliché that when a woman discusses a problem with a man the first thing he wants to do is solve it. Unfortunately this is not her aim. She wishes to air her thoughts, discover what she thinks and get closer to him. It is a cliché but nonetheless worth repeating, that women are more interested in processes and are content to view reality as emergent whereas men like to fix reality and want events with beginnings and ends and we are inclined to want to end processes as quickly as possible.

As we grow up we learn to be intolerant of uncertainty – not knowing, being lost, are feminine – and not given to reflection, characteristics which make us very unfitted for dealing with internal conflict and anxiety. As men we are wired for action and activity. This is no less so when it comes to dealing with internal conflicts. I want to explain how passivity (a universal capacity) affects the ways in which men handle these difficult internal events.

Since its inception, psychoanalysis has been preoccupied with the question of masochism. Any therapist who maintains a secure practice, in which people form a strong attachment and stay for some years, will have been repeatedly impressed with the observation that many of us repeat acts or patterns of behaviour and continue to do things which are painful or self-harming. I mean this in the most ordinary of ways rather than what might be called the extreme self-harming of slashing or cutting or indulging in life threatening sports or sexual practices. In this chapter I want to examine the meaning and function of drama and the importance of dealing with it in therapeutic practice.

Freud made a famous distinction between primary and secondary gains people get from being ill. Secondary gains are obvious ones like attention, success, affection, having no demands made on one, etc., and primary gains are concerned with the maintenance of psychological stability and security, however fragile. Although I have never found it useful in explicating primary processes, Transactional Analysis (TA), as developed by Eric Berne,[1] has always impressed me with its clarity and power in understanding and explaining secondary gains.

For those of you who are not familiar with it I should explain the basis of TA. Berne took Freud's concepts of the superego, ego and id and renamed them, respectively, Parent – Adult – Child. With this simple device (which, for these purposes, I have made more simple than it is in both theory and practice) he was able to do what psychoanalysis has never been able to do: to analyse and describe the everyday social transactions which manifested neurosis and other forms of pathology as well as normal, non-pathological relationships. It also provided, as Bateman, Brown and Pedder pointed out,[2] a powerful tool for understanding some elements of transference and counter-transference in the analytic encounter. In a major departure from Freud, Berne assumed that each ego state (as he called his trilogy) was capable of communicating with any and all of the ego states of any other person and that this could be done consciously. In other words we are all capable of behaving as parent, adult or child in relation to others and to do so in a conscious attempt to reach a particular ego state in them. Further, each ego state is capable of unconscious communication beneath the conscious or manifest one. Each communication can therefore consist of both latent and manifest elements and be aimed at eliciting particular responses from a particular ego state or combination of ego states in the object of the communication. Berne called the unit of communication a 'transaction'.

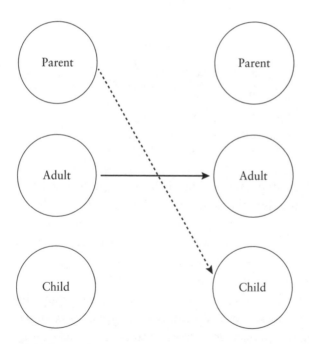

Figure 12.1   Ego states and a transaction

For example, the adult to adult request, 'Will you put your coffee cup in the dishwasher' can be heard as a parent to child statement 'You don't do enough around here' (see Figure 12.1). Of course it may also contain this latent message. The response completes the transaction, and may be similarly loaded with latent content. In fact, it is difficult to say anything that does not have latent content. When we combine these units of behaviour – transactions – with another element of TA, the 'Drama Triangle' (Figure 12.2) we have available a powerful tool for the analysis of drama and acting out in the lives of both individual and groups.

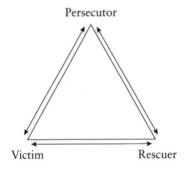

Figure 12.2   The Drama Triangle
Source: S. Karpman. 'Script drama analysis'.
Transactional Anal. Bull. April 1968. 7:26.

Stephen Karpman, who devised the triangle, opined that every drama involves the actors assuming one of the roles on the triangle and that each person has both a favourite role and the role which it is being used to defend against, but which the person inevitably ends up in at the conclusion of the game.

In Berne's theory, we see the first systematic account of the role of drama in people's lives, as well as tools for understanding it. These tools possess a face validity and explanatory power which the analytic concepts of 'repetition compulsion', 'return of the repressed', primary and secondary gains and 'acting out' simply cannot match (although the gains are undeniably matched in what they lose to subtlety). Although Berne and modern transactional analysts would insist that TA is an equally powerful tool for understanding primary gains it is truly an analysis of secondary gains. In the simplest terms, TA sees games, what I would call drama, as being dedicated to the maintenance of the status quo, both socially and psychologically. In other words, people's aim is to keep relationships, and the external world, the same as they are and have always been and to prevent disruption in their way of seeing and being in the world, even when these might both be painful. It is the human equivalent of the 'default setting' on your home computer.

To some, this is a definition of masochism. The difficulty with this explanation of the origin and motivations of drama is that it depends on an understanding of latent transactions, which is not so far from the Freudian notion of the unconscious; it is in the unconscious that the desire to maintain a painful status quo is held and from which dramatic behaviour is driven. What then is drama? In psychoanalytic terms I mean by it what I would mean by the term 'acting out'. Laplanche and Pontalis' explanation of Freud's definition (insofar as it is of interest here) is as follows:

> action in which the subject, in the grip of his unconscious wishes and phantasies, relives these in the present with a sensation of immediacy which is heightened by his refusal to recognize their source and their repetitive character.[3]

I have to say that I use a fairly broad definition of acting out in that I see it as the acting out of transferential impulses and the substitution of action for remembering. For me it includes many forms of behaviour which are employed to avoid anxiety and internal conflict evoked by the work of analysis or therapy instead of working on the anxiety or conflict in the analytic process. I do not see all forms of acting out as being the result of transference. In fact, in everyday life, 'acting out' is the normal dramas which people compulsively repeat in their relationships, and it has the same aims, the avoidance and management of anxiety. The objective of the analytic process (from a very old fashioned point of view) is to bring everything into the transference and in this case every acting out, even when it is a repetition of behaviour long predating the analysis, would be seen as an expression of acting out of the transference. I prefer to think of acting out as the enacting of any impulsive or compulsive behaviour in everyday life, whether or not they are linked to the transference. Personally I am gratified when a piece of repetitive dramatic behaviour, which compels the person into treatment, gives way to therapeutic work even if it is related only to the past and/or its present players and not the transference. I realize that my working definition conflates the compulsion to repeat, the return of the repressed and acting out in the formal sense. Although this might lack intellectual rigour, it provides a basis for useful therapeutic intervention which provides more efficacy and satisfaction than rigour.

In terms of TA (and for me psychoanalysis) drama occurs when someone repeatedly falls into one of the roles on the triangle and attempts to manoeuvre others into complementary roles. So a victim needs either a persecutor and or a rescuer. A rescuer always needs a victim and a persecutor to rescue them from and a persecutor always needs a victim. The point about these roles is that they are not simply one offs, adapted at a whim, but they are life positions which we all (according to the theory) adopt; at least those of us who are neurotic.

Drama fulfils a number of very important functions in our lives. From the point of view of the unconscious I believe its main function is to validate and legitimize certain beliefs or core constructs about the self and others and the world in general. It also functions to provide the possibility of converting trauma into triumph by setting up re-enactments of familiar painful events in the hope that this time the outcome will be different. Let me give an example which I come across often in my practice. It concerns men who continually choose relationships with women who are damaged or distressed. They take on the task of relieving the woman of her distress and depression. What is striking is that the woman never loses her distress and remains a suffering victim. The man, meanwhile, becomes increasingly resentful that all his efforts are to no avail and his rescuing position slowly mutates to that of internal victim and external persecutor. He begins to believe that she is deliberately refusing to get well, or happy or whatever it is she is supposed to do in his script. He feels that she is persecuting him. What this man is trying to do is relieve his mother of her depression so that she can begin to do what she was always supposed to do – take care of him. Unfortunately, his unconscious attachment to a neglecting, depressed and needy mother is profound. In order to relate to a woman in a different way he would have to abandon his internal mother to her fate – something which is beyond him. The fear this evokes cannot be underestimated. Fundamentally it is the fear of death for that is the fate of an infant who is without a primary carer. So long as she exists and is needy there is always the possibility of salvation for the child.

I have always had my own understanding of drama culled from years of reading and talking to patients who do it. It involves the idea of the projection of roles. In Kleinian theory the act of forcing another to take on a dramatic role would be called projective identification. For example, the writer of the script – the author or patient – experiences states of distress resulting from unconscious persecution by internal objects. This persecution can be actual attack of a humiliating, sadistic kind (in fact quite appallingly cruel) or it can be the experience of being neglected or ignored – in both cases these are continuations of early childhood or infantile experience. In non-neurotic people (and after all the differences are quantitative not qualitative – we are all fairly close to madness much of the time whether or not we know it) the outcome of this internal persecution will be experienced as inexplicable mood swings or anxieties of a sort common to us all. Usually we are not aware of the attack itself (although self-reproach is common and this can be one manifestation of it) but only of the emotional outcome. Invariably this will involve a form of anxiety which may be associated with an unpleasant feeling about the self or others.

We are all relatively powerless in the face of our internal world and primitive identifications and internalizations. How do we fight back? Who do we fight? Explicitly paranoid people can project the persecuting voices into others and fight or fly from them. In the case of psychosis the voices are 'heard' as if they come from outside – so there is an illusion. The psychotic believes the illusion and is therefore 'deluded'. For most of us the voice remains inside the head, if we hear it at all. Or we have a fantasy that the other person is 'thinking' something about us, such as that we are stupid or 'bad' in some undefined way. I will elaborate what this badness is later. If the voices or persecutors remain internal we cannot fight them. Our responses are limited to containing the distress, seeking support to get us through a temporarily difficult time or recourse to mind altering substances such as shopping, drugs, food, alcohol, medication, masturbation, sex, pornography, risk taking behaviour, etc.

There is one other alternative which can be employed in conjunction with all the above; that is drama. If by some means we can employ another to take up the role of the internal persecutor (even if we only imagine they are doing it) then we have someone we can actually fight back against! It is impossible to overestimate the psychological benefits this offers. If we can fight it we can beat it and beating it means an end to the lifelong internal persecution we have endured. If we cannot beat it we can denigrate it or otherwise reduce its status or stature in the world. If this is successful then, in effect, we dis-empower it and this is as good as a defeat. Naturally, there are certain difficulties involved in any of these processes and outcomes. The first and most obvious is that these dramatics are taking place with real people in our lives. In certain states of madness it can be entirely in the realm of fantasy as with a love affair with a star or the hatred of a public figure. As one wag put it after the demise of Richard Nixon, repeated after Mrs Thatcher met a similar fate, 'Who are we going to hate now?' The problem with real people is that they have a habit of having minds of their own and plans and dramas of their own. This can make for very unpredictable outcomes of one's dramas. One has to become more and more hostile to defend against or deny the variables which are not under one's control. Actually none of them are under control but that is another story.

These dramas are the stuff of everyday life for most people. If our own lives lack drama we apparently tune in to TV soap operas in our millions in order to keep the level of dramatic arousal to its required level! A fairly common drama, and one with which I am very familiar in my work with men in relationships, concerns the fantasy that someone close to us does not like us or is in some other way feeling antipathy or malice towards us. This will be based on the experience (not necessarily the reality) of being disrespected in some way and feeling shamed or humiliated (the infamous male 'sense of injustice' – the origin of the equally infamous 'male paranoia'). This can be precipitated by the most innocuous of stimuli which would go unnoticed even by someone else present. It can be based on no more than a fantasy, and on an act undone rather than committed. The man will quickly fall into a feeling that he has been unjustly treated and will begin an argument designed to right the wrong or get redress or vengeance. Equally often he may fall into a sulk and withdraw in a fuming, hurt rage. Feeling like a victim of an injustice he feels more than justified in persecuting the perpetrator of it. He will continue to persecute until he feels that injustice has been equalized. Such dramas can end in death or serious physical harm to women. Although the behaviour of abusive men is over determined, as we saw in the chapter on violence, from a therapeutic viewpoint it is transparently obvious to me after analysing many such men, that they are all projecting onto their partners an internal persecuting female object, almost certainly their mother and a very early one at that. It is not by any means necessary that she should have been actually persecuting in a physical way. I hinted in my last book, *Men Who Batter Women*, that one might have to begin to account for many men's extreme projections by including in any lexicon of early trauma the mother who is not attuned to the infant and whose mirroring of him is faulty or deficient. The consequences of lack of attunement, in my opinion, are potentially disastrous. An infant can be adequately serviced and simultaneously have his selfhood or potential selfhood negated. The man can end up carrying an indigestible object whom he experiences as negating his existence, of inflicting a narcissistic wound of overwhelming import. He simply cannot contain the object or the pain it inflicts (this also affords him the opportunity to backwardly project the pain and fear entailed by the beginning of the Oedipus complex). By projecting firstly the neglecting, and secondly the persecuting phallic mother into his current partner he temporarily rids himself of a poisonous internal object and the pain she causes him and simultaneously gives himself the opportunity of fighting back. A very negative maternal transference is rarely made by phallic narcissistic men in therapy (at least not with me/to me). As I said earlier, very few violently abusive men will fall into a maternal transference with a male therapist although this is not the case for 'ordinary' men whose control (however abusive it may be felt to be by their partner) is normal in averagely expectable phallic narcissism.

Another drama, which I have also come across enough times for it not to be seen as an especially deviant one, concerns men who organize sexual games involving another man or woman with them and their partner, either as voyeurs or participants. The variety I have heard more often is the one in which the husband invites another woman to have sex with him and his wife. The other variety is that in which another man is invited into the relationship. It is hard to say which is the more risky or dangerous and they are both certainly that! Stoller has said often that the most exciting sex is sex that carries the greatest degree of risk. The difficulty is managing the risk so that the excitement does not fall over into danger. Psychoanalytically, the drama involving two women is the most disturbed although the one involving another man is the most dangerous. Either way, these dramas rarely end well. Robert Hinchelwood has spoken about the role of drama in hospital communities and groups within those communities.[4] Stoller has written at length about the function of drama – particularly sexual drama and perversion in maintaining psychic health and disease.[5] Although they write for different reasons and from different perspectives, their analyses are similar. In essence they conclude that the main motivation for drama is the management of trauma or painful experience or troubling aspects of the self. They all involve the projection of central aspects of each into other people. At first sight it is hard to understand why someone would want to be involved in watching or taking part in sexual activities with their partner and another person especially given the potentially destructive intensity of jealousy in intimate relationships. This ought to be the case whether the 'stranger' is a man or a woman. I have worked with many men who produce this particular dramatic triangle. A particularly severe one involved a man who used to do it only when he had taken large amounts of cocaine, a substance to which he was seriously addicted. His drama was transparent. He would encourage his partner to take cocaine and then to go out with him and pick up men with whom she could have sex whilst he watched. On only one occasion, surprisingly, did the man also penetrate him, something which he withheld from me for some years. These episodes would always end with him having sex with his partner and he was quite clear that he was attempting to prove that he was the better man – at least consciously. The underlying trauma he was attempting to master is clear as is the fact that it did not work or it would not have been necessary to repeat the drama often. In addition, this drama was actually a subsidiary one.

The drama does not always require people to be major players. A favourite non-object relation drama (at least concretely) is the relationship with money. The story I am about to recount has links with much else that I have said already in this book and I will return to it. It concerns a very wealthy man, let us call him Colin, who was obsessed with his income and his accumulated wealth. He occupied much time every day in calculations of his 'net worth', usually in the context of his anxiety that if he were to drop dead his family would have sufficient to take care of them for the rest of their lives. It should come as no surprise to learn that this man worked in the City in a very highly paid and responsible job in global finance (now much maligned and not always fairly). His annual salary was the equivalent of most people's lifetime earnings. He is, quite simply, very rich.

Sadly, Colin was also very unhappy and anxious and filled with undifferentiated rage towards others which he was afraid he would act out. He sought me out for treatment for this homicidal rage (which he had never acted out even mildly) although it quickly became obvious that he wanted to resolve his anxiety and his depressive sadness. His depression gave way quite quickly. However, what emerged was a high level of basic insecurity and anxiety about his survival. He actually had no faith in his own 'going on being', his continued existence beyond the present moment. He functioned as if his life were about to end in death or some other catastrophe. Of course it was not difficult to make the connection between his earlier depression and his fear of death and catastrophe. The depression we had initially seen had been a mere shadow of itself and as we gradually pieced together his history we began to see its origins in his very early childhood and to understand that he had been depressed since about the age of five and it had gone unnoticed.

His anxiety about his survival was expressed in a conviction that he was going to lose all his money or that all his investments would collapse and he would be poverty stricken. I could not overstate the strength of his conviction that this was imminent. Of course it was impossible to reassure him that this was not about to happen (particularly if you had suffered the stock market crash of 2000!). This anxiety, although relatively easy to analyse and understand, proved almost intractably resistant to change; whenever he was under any sort of stress, internal or external, he would resort to calculating his net worth or calculating new ways of increasing his wealth. Mammon, the need and greed, held him in its thrall.

Its final defeat in the analytic process seems to me to illustrate many of the really important things we need to understand about drama, particularly with men. Let me outline the problems as we came to understand it. Even though we worked this problem through many times in treatment and had developed a good understanding of its roots and meaning, Colin seemed unable to stop his calculations or his anxiety about his wealth. What became apparent was that he conflated his net asset value or worth with his value as a human being. Whilst sitting in his first class plane seat he would look around at the other passengers and attempt to calculate their net worth against his own. He felt that he was a fraud and that in situations where he was with people who were worth more than him, his deception would be unmasked and he would be seen for the conman he really was. Of course, his perception that his fundamental value was contingent on his personal wealth is not particularly odd. Society (maybe even biology) has a vested interest in maintaining that conflation. The most obvious thing to say about Colin's anxiety is that it concerns loss and, moreover, of a catastrophic nature. Next, it seems clear that barring a major calamity which would affect most of humankind, he is unlikely to lose all his money or the assets in which it is invested. Additionally, it mattered not how much money he owned. In fact it seemed that the more he earned and owned the more severe his anxiety became. In part this is not so hard to understand given that the more he owned the greater he stood to lose. Whenever he acquired a large amount of money he would raise the bar on the amount he needed to feel secure. He understood that the reason he greeded so much was that he was profoundly insecure. He believed that this insecurity was financial and therefore that the solution to it was to have as much money as possible and with it would come financial security. Apart from the fact that this is impossible to achieve absolutely (as J.P. Getty said, 'you can never have enough'), it was clear that the insecurity could not possibly be financial. As his wealth increased by leaps and bounds and his insecurity and anxiety persisted he did what most of us do when presented with a difficult problem – if our solution is not working we believe that we are not doing enough of it. He concluded that he did not yet have enough money to feel secure and that what was needed was more of it. Colin's nose was pressed to the grindstone in a big way. We gradually began to understand that the resistance to giving up the fantasy of total security through financial wealth was that in this way there was at least the possibility – or the fantasy – of solving or defeating the problem. It originated in the outside world and had a solution in the outside world. The reality, which we began to appreciate, was that it existed in his inner world and there it felt to him, unconsciously, to be insoluble. The catastrophic loss he feared was the loss of all internal worth or value, and ultimately his capacity to love, a capacity about which he harboured serious and frightening doubts. The loss of all his wealth was a metaphor for the emptiness/poverty of a part of his internal world which he struggled to suppress, repress and deny. The fear of external catastrophic loss was a metaphor for going crazy; for him, we came to understand, this would mean a terrifying, debilitating depression.

I have always been a fan of Winnicott's dictum that 'the breakdown you fear is the breakdown you have already had'. For 'breakdown' one can substitute any trauma. Of course one cannot hold to this too rigidly but it is, at times, a useful enough clinical guide. Any unresolved trauma can be projected forward and dramatized if it provides the illusory possibility of resolution. Freud observed that most defence was against the idea of one's mortality and eventual death, although I believe that this is something one really only appreciates on reaching what Arundati Roy called the 'viable dieable' age (around early old age or later middle age).[6] Then it becomes an idea with which one has to grapple on a regular basis. Death is too far off for the young to be concerned with – if one ought ever to be concerned with it. What are the origins of this anxiety? Is there a universal anxiety about death, an awareness which we carry from the moment of birth? Or is this existential anxiety instead a response to early loss or similar experience which attacks the fundamental nature of attachment? In other words is it a response to trauma? The difficulty for me is that I have never seen a man who did not seem to have been traumatized even where it was impossible to determine precisely the nature of the trauma. It could be said that my sample is a self-selected and, by definition, unrepresentative one. However, I do not think it would be going too far to say that it seems we are all victims now. There were circumstances and events in his early life which adequately explain Colin's condition and his preoccupation with money even without reckoning social conditioning into the mix.

Not that there was a single epiphany. There were many on the route to his loosening his grip on the obsession with money and wealth and each was as important as the others. Gradually, as his depression gave way to the underlying rage and guilt and finally to the underlying fear and sadness he became more and more at ease and to appreciate and enjoy the wealth he had in his family and friendships.

There is another drama, so widespread as to require special mention. It is in the nature of my practice that I see a great many men who are having 'relationship difficulties'. Almost invariably the man presents as a victim of his partner. The nature of his victimization varies in the expression but the variation is usually only on the more general theme – my wife/partner is persecuting, neglectful, depriving, promiscuous/frigid or not good enough in myriad ways which leave the man feeling angry, afraid and sad. More often than not my patients are acting outside the relationship in ways that, if they were not secret, would end the relationship.

Let me give an example. It concerns a man who was referred because he had pushed his wife away from the doorway when she was attempting to prevent him leaving the house to spend the evening with his friends. She had been mildly hurt and had called the police. She refused to press charges so he was not arrested, but he was escorted from the house and did in fact spend the evening with friends. She really could not win in this situation! He spent a long time recounting the history of their marriage and how she had always been like this. She did not like him socializing with his friends and always complained when he did so. There were two children from the marriage, aged eight and three. He was a softly spoken, small man who I could not imagine being violent or threatening. He did disclose however that he could get very angry with her when she attempted to stop him going out. He insisted that he did not act this out with her other than to raise his voice. He was adamant that he never threatened, insulted her or demeaned her. In response to my question about when this drama had started he told me that it had begun when their second child was born. It quickly emerged that he had always gone out to see friends and smoke cannabis. In fact he had been doing this as often as three and sometimes four evenings a week since they were married. Prior to the birth she had questioned his behaviour but the intensity of this questioning, and demands that he change, increased markedly afterwards. His resentment and anger and feelings of victimization had increased proportionately. His self-presentation as a passive, mild mannered and softly spoken man stood in sharp counterpoint to his description of his wife as an angry harridan whose behaviour was unreasonable and at times quite mad. It was not difficult to feel some sympathy for his plight. He had always been a good provider and, when he was at home, an involved and caring father. This had been confirmed by a third party involved in the referral who was at a loss to unscramble the relationship's problems.

It is hard, too, to convey the depths of this man's distress at his plight. He simply could not understand why she was so angry with him for wanting to spend a little time with his friends.

I have deliberately chosen a relatively mild example to illustrate men's victimization at the hands and particularly mouths of their partners and the powerlessness they all report in the face of the 'attacks'. I could multiply this a hundredfold. What I intend to do is account for men's construction of this unreasonable harridan with whom they have chosen, apparently mistakenly, to have children and spend their lives. I am interested not only in their motivation for constructing such dramas of persecution and victimization but also the methods they use. Sometimes the subtlety is admirable.

This man's feelings of resentment and confusion at his wife's treatment of him served many purposes and as we unravelled them it became clear that he was as much, if not more, the author of her behaviour than was she. In particular it rapidly emerged that there was no intimacy in the relationship and had not been since the birth of the first child. He dated the onset of the real difficulties, when she started 'attacking him' as he put it, to the second birth. However it was obvious that he had been struggling since she became pregnant the first time. His trips to see his friends had been a way of withdrawing from her and protecting her from his growing resentment at his demotion down the feeding chain in the family. He was required to give more as he was receiving less and he was unable to do so without resentment and anger. It was not difficult to see that he was in a serious sulk. The point is that however much he protested the lack of intimacy in the relationship and her responsibility for it, it might have been designed to maintain his psychological stability. In brief, like many men he did not want intimacy with his wife and, more importantly, had never wanted it! What he required was control and the significant thing about the control he required was that it would enable him to have the sort of intimacy he wanted *when* he wanted it and on his terms and in his time. It requires little thought to see that this does not meet any of the requirements of intimacy in a relationship. Intimacy is the antithesis of control. It requires vulnerability, openness and disclosure in order to allow one's personal and self-boundaries to be crossed without threat and anxiety – highly feminizing.

He constantly provoked her with taunts that she was a bad wife for scolding him and that if she stopped he might want to spend more time with her. Of course if she stopped he did not change his behaviour and the cycle continued. Pathologizing her need for intimacy (the pursuing wife) shifts the focus of concern away from its more legitimate target, the man. By setting up this drama in which she becomes the bad object who has to be avoided, justifiably, he never has to face his own anxieties about intimacy and what it is that really frightens him and that he runs away from. The 'distancer' husband is fundamentally afraid of women – perhaps all men are. The secondary gains from his drama are clear. He gets to see his friends as often as he wishes and feel guilt-free about it. He gets to avoid all the onerous duties associated with being a father and running a home and having a marriage. The primary gain is fundamental. He never has to face his real anxieties about being close to a woman.

Another common example is the brother of the distancer – the frigid husband. He is usually to be found with the distancer, as sexual intimacy is simply another, but in some ways, more threatening form of contact when engaged in with a long term partner. The issue is the same. He needs to have sex, but it has to be on his terms and his time and place. Failing that, she is a 'castrating bitch' and obviously doesn't want to have sex with him. It may be true that she is not interested in the sort of sex that interests him. More than likely she would like some sort of emotional intimacy as a forerunner to genital contact – some sexual intimacy rather than simply fucking. Lest I be thought sexist here let me say that I know that women also sometimes like to just fuck. In an intimate relationship I like to think that this is possible and that a man who is not intimacy phobic will be happy to follow her agenda just as she is happy, at times, to follow his. The truth is that many men I have worked with are reduced to impotence by a woman wanting sex. It is simply not feminine for a woman to want to be, or at least share, in control of a couple's sexual relationship. As women will say, in so many words, they have never had a sex life of their own, they have always had their partner's sex life. Sex occurs when he wants it, where he wants it and how he wants it. The strategies men use to maintain their control are not always subtle and repetitive drama plays a large part. I recall one man who would always create a reason to never go to bed at the same time as his partner so that she would always be asleep when he eventually did so. He had already established sufficient control that he had managed to define the bed as the only location in which sex could happen in spite of her many protests. Often he would manage to provoke a minor disagreement so that the relationship was frosty late at night. I could multiply the strategies many times but suffice to

say they all served the same purpose. Whenever a man tells me
that he does not have as much sex as he wishes because of his
partner's sexual problems I now automatically make the silent
interpretation that he is afraid of sexual intimacy. Naturally, I
do not articulate this without some preparation.

I hope I have said enough about drama and its motivations
to enable the reader to see beneath the manifest content and to
have confidence in his understanding of his plight. In treatment,
sooner or later the difficulties will be enacted in the transference.
All it requires is patience. My thoughts about drama and the
way men dramatize in relationships has led me, over the years,
to develop a particular way of intervening which I have found
useful in situations where the space between a couple is so full
of mad projections that any form of reality testing or analytic
reflection seems impossible. It is based on a model I have
developed from my work with the concept of drama – I call it
the Mad Hypothesis.

13
The Mad Hypothesis

The Mad Hypothesis occupies a prominent place in all my groupwork and informs a lot of my activity in individual work. Initially I used it only in men's groups but then it gained a foothold in my mixed gender groups as men transferred from one to the other and emigrated with the concept, so to speak. It has proven to be so useful that I intend to devote a book to it but set out the idea here because it has proven especially useful in my work with men. At first glance it does not seem very psychodynamic or analytic but I hope to show otherwise. I initially developed it in working with men who were involved in relationships which were full of 'malignant mirroring'. This is a situation in which two people reflect each other as monsters by repeatedly articulating how bad they each think the other is. The relationship is full of the accusative form – YOU! It is as if each holds up to the other a mirror in which the reflection projected is of someone who is irredeemably bad. The image one sees of oneself is of someone so bad that it is unrecognizable and indigestible. To identify with it would involve metabolizing so much madness and/or badness that self-destruction would seem to be the only escape from the guilt. What I learned from working with men in such relationships is that reality testing is impossible. Each member of the couple is struggling to locate the badness or madness in the relationship in the other. It is a very damaging and dangerous form of splitting and leaves each person feeling very disturbed as they fail to either project the madness or to own it. The result is that the space between the couple is full of crazy projections which cannot be subjected to reality testing – even of the 'cut the baby in half' nature. The mad hypothesis became a way for a man to learn how to prevent the frequent and damaging quarrels, rows and violence that characterizes such relationships.

At its simplest the mad hypothesis is expressed as follows:

> You are responsible for everything that is wrong with your relationship including any behaviour of your partner which you use to justify, excuse or in any other way account for your own behaviour towards her or the world in general.

In *Men Who Batter Women* this was referred to as the working hypothesis. It has become the mad hypothesis because so many people said it was mad! Later, as I used it in my routine therapeutic work with non-abusers and with women, I changed it to include everything that was wrong with the person's life, not only their relationship, without any apparent loss of clarity, precision, utility or efficacy. I will describe how it is used in work with both abusive and non-abusive men. Although I am drawing a distinction here I want to reiterate that I regard the differences between substantiated abusing/controlling and non-abusing/controlling men to be quantitative, not qualitative and that anything I say can be successfully applied to all.

Of course it is a mad idea. Simply on the face of it, it seems to portray the woman as no more than a cipher, a two dimensional cut-out in the man's world and as an object without desire or agency. Again, on the face of it we know this cannot be so even though we know from the speaking bitterness literature of the women's movement that many women actually experience themselves in just this way after years of abuse from the men they live with. However, as Chapter 8 ('The Use of an Object') will have made clear, it is not at all mad to hypothesize that a man will view his partner as a two dimensional object suitable for use.

I actually tell abusive men this hypothesis in the very first assessment session and I point out that it is mad because we all know that there are two people in a relationship. Actually, few violent men know what a relationship is – they have no internal model of a couple and usually lack a theory of mind from which they can perceive their partner. Generally he will regard her as a servant, as someone who is there simply to fulfil his needs and meet his expectations. The sad reality is that the mad hypothesis is not so mad as it seems. It is really a sleight of hand, an acceptable, seeming lie to encourage the man to enter treatment. Actually it is not a new idea at all. Those of you who are familiar with Freud will recognize that the mad hypothesis is a condensation of his ideas concerning the primary and secondary gains from illness.[1]

I cannot over-emphasize the centrality or the importance to me of this hypothesis in my work with men's relationships with women. Without it the work I do would be so different as to be unrecognizable. It has become a commonplace for men and women in treatment groups with me to mention 'the mad hypothesis'. It is extremely rewarding to my narcissism when they say, as they do, that the mad hypothesis has actually 'saved their lives' in so many different ways. The method of use is transparently simple. It can also be applied by anyone in any difficult situation, not simply when violence or aggression is involved or threatened – in fact it is not an unreasonable premise on which to base any form of treatment for emotional distress, most especially with the 'worried well'. When the man is in difficulty (in fact when any one of us is in difficulty) he will usually define himself as a victim of his partner. He will invariably be experiencing a sense of injustice, for which of us does not when we feel we are being victimized. In such circumstances we invariably become preoccupied with the motives and behaviour of our perceived persecutor. I usually describe it to patients as similar to the preparation of a story board for a film in which all the major events of the film are represented by a picture. From the very first picture, much, if not all, of the events that follow are given a set of meanings which are limited by that first picture. From his perspective she has done something to him which he constructs as persecuting, as in the coffee cup incident (see Chapter 6). Seen from the first picture, both his sense of injustice and his revenge are fully justified, understandable and legitimate, but his distress, his sense of injustice and his blaming of his partner has little or nothing to do with her behaviour. This cannot be overemphasized with controlling/abusive men. Give an inch and they will take a mile! I know this will sound harsh to many but abusive men, like all men, have used every explanation they can think of to explain their own and their partner's behaviour – but without success or they would not be in my office. I introduce the mad hypothesis to the man by simply asking him what is the missing picture before the one that he uses to begin his narrative. In other words, 'what did you do to make her do what she is doing to you in the first picture and which defines you as her victim'. It is at this point that the madness of the hypothesis becomes clear. In effect I am saying to him that he is not only responsible for his own behaviour but also for any behaviour of hers which he uses to justify any of his treatment of her. The mad hypothesis emerged out of the need for a rapid, radical intervention with violent men. Speed is essential; there are real people being hurt so long as the man continues to behave in his habitual ways, and this often includes children, whether or not they are the targets of the violence. Permanent damage results from simply being raised in such a family.

The mad hypothesis has been very successful with violent offenders to women. On the face of it this is quite hard to explain. Most of these men have been to the very limit to avoid any suggestion that they are in any way responsible for their own behaviour. In fact every justification or excuse, every account, they give is intended to achieve this one simple end: to deny responsibility. Why then should they take so readily to an idea which states explicitly that not only are they fully responsible for their own behaviour, but also for their victims? Moreover, a victim who, until that moment, they had seen as their persecutor.

I think the first answer is that it confirms what they already know; that they are, in fact, responsible for pretty much everything that has gone wrong in the relationship. They know they are responsible for their violent and abusive behaviour but they are unable to acknowledge it either to themselves or their partners. The main reason for this is, as Freud would have put it, the counter-transference. Their self-love or narcissism will not allow such a massive re-organization of the self-image. Basically they would have to admit that they are in some important senses, not a very nice person. This would involve too much guilt, shame, self-loathing and remorse. What the mad hypothesis allows is for them to acknowledge what they know to be the truth but in the presence of an 'expert' (who also happens to not be a woman!) who is simultaneously telling them that it is simply an experiment and not really the truth at all. I frequently attach it to a very simple description of systems theory and say something to the effect that it doesn't matter very much where we intervene in the system because a change in any of its components will change the whole system anyway. Naturally, not all men take to this readily. At this point some will say something to the effect that it isn't fair that he should take all the blame and that one of the reasons he abuses is that she will never acknowledge she is in the wrong and he gets blamed for everything. Of course this is nonsense. The fact is that he is swollen with guilt about his abusiveness and consequently believes himself to be persecuted by his victim. This is the only way he can account for his guilt ('she is blaming me all the time') and one of the few ways he can account for his abusive behaviour. I'm usually content when men respond in this way because it leads us so effortlessly into his 'sense of injustice'.

Another reason why men are willing to work with the mad hypothesis is that it immediately offers a paradigm which gives them the experience of being in control (again!) and of being able to wield an influence on events which, up until that moment, they had felt were out of control. It should come as no surprise that I have found it to be a very helpful diagnostic tool insofar as it focuses me on the question of the primary and secondary gains from the symptom or 'illness'.

There is one important caveat; although I have no doubt that many women unconsciously seek out abusive partners particularly when they have grown up in a home in which their father abused their mother, this in no way indicates that they have a conscious wish to be abused or enjoy it when it happens, any more than rape fantasies indicate a wish to be raped. Nobody enjoys being abused however validating it may be for the unconscious weltanschauung.

My experience is that most people already use the mad hypothesis. There is one important difference in this use – in most people's version they are the victim of someone else who is responsible not only for their own behaviour but also 'mine'. In their accounts 'my behaviour' is a reaction to their provocation.

Let me illustrate with some examples. I could give many from my work with women, but in keeping with the goal of this work I shall present only from my work with men.

Take the well known case of the 'pursuer wife and the distancer husband'. She has it that no matter how hard she tries to get close to him he always backs away; she feels frustrated and deprived. He has it that she never allows him to get close because she it always trying to force him to be close to her and he feels swamped and devoured. Systemically this is rather simple. Each is causing the other's behaviour and each is blaming the other. He pathologizes her need for intimacy, it's neurotic, and she pathologizes his fear of intimacy, probably accurately. Who started it? is a wholly irrelevant question. Do they want to change it? is the issue. Actually in my work it is usually whether *he* wants to change it. The solution is simple. He has to begin to approach her and do the analytic work required to confront his fear of intimacy.

Or take the case of the man who cannot have a conversation with his wife or listen to her because she is always repeating herself and getting angry with him. The question 'What do you do to make her repeat herself and get angry with you?' usually elicits the simple answer that he does not listen to her so that what he sees as an effect is actually a cause. This is usually referred to by men as the 'nagging' issue. Nagging is what women do to men after men have decided, unilaterally, that the conversation is over.

The informed reader will perhaps have begun to recognize the phenomenon familiar to communication theorists of 'the solution which is the problem'. This is the idea that when someone recognizes a problem they usually attempt to solve it by doing more of what they have always done without recognizing that this is the problem (those interested should take a look at *Change* by Watzlawick et al.[2]).

Take the case of the man who complained that his wife did not want to have sex with him as often as he wanted. When asked if she ever requested sex the reply was 'not for a very long time'. Again with a little probing it became evident that when she had made a request he had never responded positively. In effect his wife had never had any sex life except his. Is it any wonder she was less than compliant? This is a good example of a man using a woman as a sexual object. It was evident he was afraid of sexual intimacy.

Let's look at a more complex example. This concerns a man who had not had a foreign holiday with his family for years because neither he nor his wife or children had up-to-date passports. He had reproached his wife constantly with her failure to renew them. He worked hard outside the home whilst she was a full time wife and mother. He thought it not unreasonable that she should do what was required to see to the renewal. His reproaches had not always been quiet or non-intimidating. She suffered from a severe flight phobia and it was clear what was her investment in not having passports. His attitude to her phobia (she had more complex depressive problems also) was nothing short of contempt for her frailty and vulnerability (a mirror of his attitude to his own). She saw this as exactly the sort of support she had received from him on the odd occasions they had flown when they had passports. He had effectively abandoned her emotionally as soon as they booked a holiday whilst she went through days of panic and depression at the prospect of flying. This lack of sensitivity and empathy, his emotional coldness, was typical of his treatment of her in their marriage. He had consistently rejected her attempts at intimacy to the point where she had built a life that did not involve him. Of course he complained bitterly about being excluded by her activities and blamed her for the lack of intimacy – he had never had to consider that this was his problem and that he had constructed a solution which enabled him to simultaneously avoid his fears and project the guilt and blame.

Any doubts I might have held about the 'mad hypothesis' were dispelled in a group when its validity was being discussed in critical terms. The central attack concerned the majority feeling in the group that most of their behaviour was caused by their partner's treatment of them. I made a banal comment about how much they liked to occupy the victim position and have it validated by other members when it suddenly occurred to me that they were all, already, using the hypothesis except that in their version it was their partner who was responsible for his behaviour as well as her own. Not without some pleasure at my cleverness I pointed this out and it provoked gales of laughter when I suggested that since they already believed the mad hypothesis was valid all I was suggesting was that they reverse it! I have repeated this observation many times in my individual work with men and women – with similar positive outcomes.

14
Conclusion – Is there a Cure for Masculinity?

This book has not been about abusers, except insofar as it is about men. It is however, unusual in that I have set out to describe how I work with men from a psychodynamic model which is informed by almost 30 years of working with abusive men. In that time I have discovered that abusive men and others are pretty much the same or are certainly more alike than they are different. It goes without saying that everything in this book has been learned in the clinical setting; in treating men who have presented with various forms of the disorders of masculinity which seem most common. These are initially presented as behaviour problems which are disturbing to others as well as being self-destructive.

What has been the focus of my interest here is the relationship between these behaviours and the whole idea of masculinity. What precisely is it? Of course one might as well ask what is gender identity? Sex is a given – at least in name. We are born male or female (or something other) but these categories are givens and are joined according to one's anatomy at birth. However, what they signify is not given apart from primary sexual characteristics like penis and testes or vagina or breasts or menstruation etc. Masculinity and femininity are of a different order. They, too, depend largely on anatomy at birth. However, unlike sex, male or female, they are empty categories which depend entirely on social construction. There are those who believe that any masculinity has a historical and cultural specificity, that it has a time and a place – which means that there is a multiplicity of masculinities which may share no more than a piece of anatomy. Although I believe this to be true about elements of masculinity I take issue on the major point. I believe there is a form of masculinity which is a-historical, a-cultural and monolithic. I realize that this comes perilously close to arguing that there is something innate about masculinity, which I actually do not believe. In this book I have called the trans-cultural, trans-historical masculinity the big M and located its origins in phallic narcissism and the defensive over-valuation of the penis in the face of underlying unresolved trauma. In effect I have defined masculinity, as represented here, as a defence against distress.

I have presented a case study of a lifelong cross-dresser to illustrate certain connections between shame, masculinity and perversion. I could have multiplied his story tenfold to illustrate the point I want to make – that masculinity is deeply problematic for most men. Underlying it is a deep sense of loss and grief, even in 'normal' men, that is left from the separation and dis-identification from the mother, even without earlier experiences of loss or trauma. Masculinity is developed during the subsequent phallic phase and it has its roots in the shame and failure which are all too apparent then. The subsequent difficulties in coming to terms with sexual difference and the absence of a penis on a woman provide all that is needed to lay the foundation for 'active' masculinity and the desire to act out that is precipitated by shaming and humiliations experiences. Further case histories from my cross-dressers group would have served to re-enforce the point.

I could have written about Carl who had great difficulty in maintaining a relationship with a woman. All his life he had involved himself in homosexual activities, but only once involving full anal intercourse when he was a young man. It subsequently became clear that his gay episodes were closely connected to incidents in which he felt he had been unfairly attacked or persecuted by his female partner. His experience of being castrated (dissed, bitched, shamed, humiliated) would echo a familiar theme in the stories contained in this book. It required little work to establish that his gay episodes engendered a feeling in him of being more of a man than the other man. A very interesting, if transparent triumph over his experience of the shame and humiliation of his girlfriend's castration and emasculation of him.

His masturbatory activity consisted of his cross-dressing in female clothes and masturbating whilst looking at himself in the mirror. He would attempt to arrange the mirror in such a way that he was unable to see his own face but could see his genitals and his erect penis. This could not be a clearer expression of his denial of the absence of a penis on a woman and his triumph over his castration anxiety.

Or I could have written about Eric, a highly successful, very rich 'alpha' male. Like Carl he came to me when he was going through a very painful separation from his wife of ten years following her infidelity. He had become very depressed and defeated. He had lost interest in work and relationships. He had made a number of very serious suicide attempts which he had been lucky to survive. He had been very disappointed to have revived from the last attempt. He had gone to inordinate lengths to prevent discovery and been thwarted by pure chance.

Eric's mother had shamed and humiliated him for as long as he had a memory – from about age two – and since age six Eric had been fixated on cross-dressing and bondage. This had lasted until about age 16 but had metamorphosed during the ten years of its greatest intensity. From being associated with an undifferentiated state of excitement and arousal – but without erection whilst wearing his mother's underwear – it had become full blown masturbation at the onset of puberty. This cross-dressing and bondage accompanying masturbation to orgasm whilst in his mother's underclothes had begun its life when he had seen the cover of a true crime magazine which showed a picture of an attractive and obviously terrified young women tied and bound and dressed in underwear. A man, who had obviously bound her, was standing over and pointing his gun at her.

Then there is Richard who had cross-dressed all his life since his teenage years. He was in middle age when he came to me. His marriage was in a terminal state. His wife was having an affair with a man whom he knew and he could not forgive her. He insisted he still loved her. It mattered little that he had not wanted to make love with her for years. In fact he had basically lost interest in her sexually after the birth of their two sons. The children were now young adults.

Richard had been abandoned by his mother at the age of two and left in the care of a devoted and loving, but very passive and frequently absent businessman father. He hated his mother with a passion. He could not talk about her without references to killing her and referred to her as that bitch or cunt. Unsurprisingly he had little faith in mothers and this had been transferred without resistance to his own wife as she raised their children. The difficulties the children were now facing as they became independent (and these were not inconsiderable and sometimes criminal) he blamed entirely on her failure. His cross-dressing did not always involve masturbation. In fact he maintained that this had never been its main motivation. As he described it: 'When I am dressed as a woman I feel completely relaxed. It's the only time I don't feel like killing someone.'

We know that one of the major characteristics of perverse men is that they idealize women. Of course this is a primitive defence against envy, fear and hatred with associated annihilation anxiety. The idealization is usually very thin – it is not hard to discern the underlying contempt and denigration which is a further line of defence against envy. I recall a man who had been sent to boarding school at age six in order, as his father put it, to make a man of him. As you would expect he was deeply traumatized by this and his emotional growth was severely impaired. He was a compulsive seducer of women who was usually 'in relationship' with at least five women. In his Casanova like pursuit of women he insisted he was attempting to find a partner with whom he could settle down and have children. In fact it was mainly in order to satisfy his desire for casual sex. He was unable to sustain a relationship and could not masturbate – he thought men who masturbate are less than real men. His solution was to masturbate inside women – and this was usually necessary three or four times a week. His manic pursuit of women had the qualities of a military campaign. It required the equivalent of a master of wine's cellar notebook. Without his notes, he admitted, he would get the different women confused and therefore needed to check who he was meeting each time. After a number of meetings he would be able to differentiate individuals from the pack.

One does not need dynamic insight to recognize a manic defence in operation. A manic defence is a strategy in which a form of hyperactivity is used to blot out depression. In the extreme it is a psychotic condition. Klein said that the manic defence is based on the omnipotent idea that any amount of damage to the object can be repaired and there was no doubt that this man was aware of his hatred of women.

A final example could be described as almost 'normal'. It was a man who came to me in the middle of an extreme marital crisis brought on by his systematic emotional abuse of his wife. It emerged initially that he used to wear her underwear during any separations from her. Once he had made this connection with his separation anxiety he seemed satisfied that the issue was closed and did not mention it again for about two years.

His behaviour is very close to the 'normal' male fetish with female lingerie but with the addition that he gained pleasure from wearing it. The core meaning of this behaviour was so transparent because he only acted it out when he was separated from his wife and children and felt alone and lonely. At its simplest, it was a defence against separation anxiety. Of course it raises further interesting questions, such as how does the wearing of his wife's underwear protect him from his fears of abandonment and loss? What is the role of sexuality and eroticism in this process? The answers are fairly simple. By putting himself in her 'skin' she cannot leave him. By becoming sexually aroused he is potent, not vulnerable. He has triumphed by converting the undeniable 'loss' into a source of excitement, not fear. More importantly, what does it say about masculinity that all of these men in some way play around with their gender identity, for that is what they were doing, and still identify strongly as men and male? One might be forgiven for thinking that such behaviour would evoke anxiety at the least and homosexual anxiety at worst.

What can we say about these very different and yet very similar men? They represent a biased sample insofar as they all entered long term psychoanalytic therapy with the aim of relieving some distressing symptom or anxiety. However, in no case did they present their gender conflicts as problematic until quite late in treatment. In fact not all regard their gender bending behaviour as problematic even deep into treatment. I have worked with many men who have transsexual or transvestite fantasies or masturbatory activities. The work of the well known sexologists was immensely helpful, particularly Stoller. However, as in all these things there is no substitute for experience.

I want to point out something that is commonplace for anyone practising analytic therapy: desire is very problematic for most people. By this I do not want to confuse desire with its object, which is more about the operationalization of desire into want or consumption – the point where satisfaction, or at least the illusion of it, is uppermost. I am referring to desire without content and in this raw state it is more akin to anxiety but is not anxiety. As the Buddha said, 'All desire is pain.' I remember one of my analysts pointing out that I seemed unable to enjoy desiring for its own sake. At the time this was like hearing a haiku. It sounded poetic but made no sense. Understanding it was a liberation for me as it proved subsequently to be for many of the people I work with.

However, to return to masculinity. The point I am making is that desire is central to its definition. Men are constructed as desiring objects. Freud's despairing 'what do women want' reads like a cry in the wilderness of unsatisfied desire. There is little doubt that men are the lucky gender when it comes to concretizing desire. Freud's question is not so much a reflection of women's lack of desire; it is not, as one wag put it, 'what do women want' but 'do they want?' In other words Freud assumed the desire but despaired of ever knowing what might satisfy it. Women, as received wisdom has it, are constructed as the objects of desire. It certainly seems that men perceive them in this way or expect them to behave in concordance with such a construction by, for example, wanting to be dominated by them. My problem is not so much what men desire as much as it is to answer the more basic question of what desire is. I have neither the time nor the intellect to do this question justice as have many others.[1] I content myself with the notion that 'desire is life' and that its absence is the psychological equivalent of death – what might be thought of as an extreme state of depression or anxiety.

For me this is a practical and clinically effective solution to the conundrum that is desire and to the 'normally deviant' and occasionally extreme ways that men have of expressing it. It also explains Freud's statement that perversion is the negative of neurosis – although I prefer to see is as the negative of loss, grief, anxiety and depression. When I think of my patients who have gone through suicidal crisis, or in rare cases actually suicided, I would not describe them as having suffered from a wish to die. They all wished to stop suffering (and other more confused motives) but it made no sense to see them as being driven by a death instinct. What did make sense in almost all cases was that they were suffering intolerably because they had experienced the pain of unbearable loss and had no desire to go on. I believe that desire is fundamentally the wish to experience being safe and protected – an absence of danger and no anxiety, peace of mind. I am aware that it would be very easy to confuse this with either a wish to return to the breast, the womb (birth trauma) or to the eternity from which we came (death instinct) but that is not what it represents to me or to my patients. This presents men with a dilemma, the unsatisfactory resolution of which formed part of the bedrock of what they think of as masculinity and which goes a long way to accounting for the apparently perverse and gender challenging behaviour which has formed the larger part of this book. This gets me back to the underlying theme; that masculinity is constructed out of phallic narcissistic defences against an underlying basic fault deriving from the loss of and separation from the maternal or primary object.

Baldly, and dynamically as opposed to concretely, I understand masculinity to be a set of defences against attachment anxieties and anxieties about loss, either already suffered or feared. These anxieties arise during the separation/individuation phase of development and reach their apogee during the onset of the phallic phase – the beginning of the Oedipus complex. This marks the beginning of the construction of phallic narcissistic masculinity.

I think it is clear from the histories here that the lives of these men were shaped by experiences of profound loss and or emotional/physical trauma. In fact, as I have said earlier, all my male patients have endured and adapted to such experience.

As a result, the phallic phase and the discovery of the comfort of the penis and the promise of the identification with the fantasy of the father leads to a masculinity designed to mask the underlying shame of feeling unlovable, vulnerable and helpless. This denied shame will provide the world with a ready-to-hand tool for shaping masculinity and determining just what can be said to constitute it for the rest of a man's life. Masculinity is fundamentally a defence against that underlying vulnerability –

and subsequently the denial of sexual difference. I hope I am not being too intellectual if I point out that masculinity, as I model it, is predicated on the denial of sexual difference – the denial of the woman's absent penis (and so, of course, any possibility of a masculinity which could be construed as feminine). So, the defences are constructed as the opposite of the vulnerability and helplessness and are the quintessence of phallic and narcissistic. They emphasize potency, strength, fearlessness, carelessness about safety (courage and bravery, risk taking – self-destructiveness) and the denial of attachment needs, total independence. Whenever men are threatened with a shaming or humiliating experience – and this is anything that will make them feel afraid or otherwise vulnerable – most men will escalate their defences; that is, will become determinedly more masculine, whatever that means for him in their idiosyncratic construction of it. He may masturbate, use pornography, cross-dress, seek out a gay experience, drink, gamble, be unfaithful, see a prostitute or engage in other forms of risky sexuality. Some men will seek to construct lives which are 'unmistakably' masculine so that the possibility of their being considered vulnerable will simply never be considered. One has only to think of the number of world champion boxers (Mike Tyson is the only example one needs) who collapse and self-destruct after retirement to see precisely how much of a hold the necessity to be strong can have on a damaged and deeply vulnerable personality. It could be said that masculinity is not only based on a lie, but that it is a lie. It is not such a step from that to employing dishonesty in everyday life as a man attempts to hide the more unacceptable parts of his phallic masculinity (I see this particularly in political life and in the lives of all men who are ambitious for success and power).

So, is there a 'cure'? Is there an illness? Is masculinity a sickness? I think it is clear that I believe that masculinity can become a sickness in its more extreme exemplars and can be profoundly distressing even in its normal ones. I ask you to imagine, what might a non-masculine man look like? It will be very difficult to find a model in any successful position, whether religion, business, the arts, politics, medicine or sport. Although it is not necessarily so, a lot of ambition is required to be successful in those activities and ambition is clearly phallic narcissistic. Success comes to some as a by-product of doing something they enjoy and are also very good at without it ever having been an objective. As to a cure, clearly, I believe there to be one. Analytic psychotherapy is a cure and in my practice this is also combined with the effective use of the Mad Hypothesis. Using it appropriately can help men to develop the psychic muscle to tolerate depression, sadness and loss, vulnerability and fear which are fundamental for subverting phallic masculinity. Central to this is the ability to tolerate shame and humiliation without acting out or escalating the masculine defence. The development of this one capacity will subvert any 'masculine' identity, however rigid or traumatized. With perversion this is relatively simple. All that is required is patience, time, silence and speech. Every articulated thought or experience in the presence of a non-judgemental therapist or analyst, who is not prone to embarrassment himself, will develop just a little more space for the acceptance of a masculinity which is not driven by the need to fight or fuck or compete. When a man recognizes that he is the author of his own narrative and understands why he writes the narrative he is living he is most of the way to developing an identity which is not governed by the need to get rich, fight or fuck.

One thing is clear to me. Every major non-geological disaster in history has been man made, from climate change to credit crunch and from warfare to genocide. Masculinity is not fit for purpose if that purpose is to ensure the survival of the human race. Men's denial of vulnerability and the need to consume and acquire are intricately connected. The conflation of wealth, power, possessions and status, thence to potency are fundamentally man constructed and man driven. It would seem we men are willing to do anything to get as far away as possible from that underlying fragility and that we are driven by short term goals and not long term consequences.

Postscript

Hopefully the reader will have retained sufficient interest to want to know what happened to the man with whom I began this book.

When he returned to the next and final session, it was to inform me, with the largest of triumphant grins that after our session when I had told him he would probably always be impotent, he had gone home and had sex with his wife five (yes, *five*) times that night and that they had basically spent the weekend in bed. I lost no time in informing him that this was probably a temporary reaction to the previous session and that nothing he had said had changed my conclusion and that he had simply better get used to the idea. He disagreed strongly. He did shake my hand as he left.

Some years later I had a call from him in which he thanked me profusely for saving his marriage and his career. He was now the proud father of three children and had been promoted twice to a very senior position in the government agency in which he worked. He told me that he had been so furious with me that he had not been able to think clearly about what happened or why his behaviour changed so radically but that after a couple of years it had become clear to him. The understanding had not caused a regression but had simply led to his being very grateful to me for taking such a radical step.

I am sure you can work out what happened here. I used his phallic narcissism against him by using it to fuel a response to a challenge from me. I made the consequences of failure so serious that he had not been able to contemplate it unconsciously. He had to defeat me, even if it meant getting 'well'.

Would I do this again in the same circumstances? Even though my intervention had a profound and beneficial effect on the man's life the answer is, probably not. You may be able to work out why.

Appendix

This was a suggested programme for expectant fathers which we believed could prevent much marital breakdown and mental distress for families. Unfortunately it was not taken up by Sure Start.

Fathers Figured?

The aim of this programme:

Helping men work through the complex issues connected with becoming a father.

Helping men see fatherhood as an enriching experience that involves their full, active and positive contribution.

Reducing the emotional distress and, often, the violence and abuse that men inflict on their partners during pregnancy and the first year after birth.

Why is it needed?

Research and experience clearly indicate that much of the origin of marital breakdown and men's abusive behaviour in families begins with the first pregnancy and the birth of children.

Many, if not most, men are simply not prepared for the impact of a new life on their relationship with their partner.

Even planned pregnancies that have been discussed and desired can create anxiety and depression in the prospective father.

40% of pregnancies are unplanned.

Much of the anxiety about the arrival of the baby is displaced onto gathering together the practical resources needed.

Most antenatal classes focus on the practical issues related to the birth.

However, being truly prepared involves the gathering of internal, emotional and psychological resources.

Some men exhibit a wide range of destructive responses as anxiety and depression set in.

As many as 20% of pregnant women are assaulted by their partners. A far higher proportion is emotionally and psychologically abused.

If there are children already in the family, up to 90% of them will witness the violence and up to 50% will also be abused by the father.

Other forms of acting out include infidelity, abuse of alcohol or drugs, withdrawal from family, compulsive working, use of pornography, visits to prostitutes.

The incidence of marital breakdown in the time of pregnancy and during the first year after the birth points to childbirth as a significant cause of marital failure.

What will Fathers Figured do?

We provide a groupwork environment that helps each participant to:

Recognize and respond to the often negative impact of pregnancy and birth on their relationship with their partner.

Recognize and respond to any behavioural changes since the pregnancy started and the impact this is having on other family members.

Deal with the impact of finding himself in a situation where he is suddenly getting much less from his partner.

Adjust to a situation where he has to provide much more not only to his partner but also to the new baby.

Face up to the powerful, unresolved anxieties connected with his own childhood and his own experience of being parented.

Come to terms with any feelings of jealousy he has towards his newborn child.

Come to terms with any desire he has to be rid of the child.

Examine how he feels about being the husband or partner of a mother.

Consider the extent to which he is subject to cultural pressures to behave in a 'manly' way and not be open about anxiety or depressive feelings for fear of being shamed or humiliated by his peers.

If not handled sensitively this complex mixture of reactions at what is anyway a stressful time in life, can lead to a damaging breakdown of the marriage or relationship and to the loss of connection and contact between fathers and children.

What will happen on the programme?

The programme will be in two parts.

The first part will be semi-structured and run for 30 weeks. It will be an open group with a maximum of eight participants. There will be a range of pre-determined topics based on our knowledge of the issues men face, but there will be some flexibility to deal with immediate issues particularly if these place someone in danger. A range of groupwork techniques will be used in order to stimulate and aid discussion. Topics and activities will include:

- Role of being a father – myths and reality.
- Keeping pregnancy logs – what men are experiencing, what they think others, particularly their partner, is experiencing, what they think the baby is experiencing.
- Responding to the needs of the baby.
- Responding to the needs of their partner.
- 28% of men have never changed their baby's nappy. Why?
- Responding to the impact of pregnancy and birth on his relationship with his partner.
- Being pregnant is the second most vulnerable time for a woman to be assaulted by her partner. Why?
- What about sex?
- How can you make and sustain changes?

The second part of the programme is unstructured. There will be an open agenda around the issues of fatherhood and parenting.

Who is the programme suitable for?

The programme is available to men whose partner is pregnant or within the early years after a birth.

Some men may be aware of the link between their anxiety and their partner's pregnancy, but most will not.

Ways in which men begin behaving out of character include:

- Overworking and worries about job security.
- Alcohol or drug abuse.
- Gambling.
- Being unfaithful, visiting prostitutes, using pornography.
- Become withdrawn and uncommunicative.
- Loss of interest in relationship or intimacy.
- Abuse and physical violence directed at their partner and the unborn or newborn baby.

It is often hard for a man to acknowledge that he is experiencing difficulty. This may involve recognizing particular cultural or ethnic factors that will be of particular importance in helping the man to overcome his resistance to disclosing or addressing his difficulties.

Where it is possible and safe to do so, we attempt to enlist the support of the mother or mother to be in encouraging and supporting her partner to join a Fathers Figured programme.

The maladaptive ways of managing anxiety set out above, can be compounded by the absence of social and familial support particularly in migrant communities or other communities who are unable for a variety of reasons to access community resources.

How will the programme be delivered?

There will be a 30 session semi-structured groupwork programme followed by an open unstructured module of undetermined length.

There will be a maximum of eight participants.

Notes

1 Introduction – Clinical Case Studies

1. A. Jukes. *Why Men Hate Women*. 1993. Free Association Books.
2. J. McDougall. *A Plea for a Measure of Abnormality*. 1992. Routledge.
3. S. Frosh. *Sexual Difference, Masculinity and Psychoanalysis*. 1994. Routledge.
4. A. Jukes. *Men Who Batter Women*. 1999. Routledge.

There are other theories about masculinity and men which are worth a look and will stimulate further reading:

R. Connell. *Masculinities*. 1995. Cambridge, Polity.

N. Duffell. *The Making of Them*. 2000. Lone Arrow Press. A moving study of the effects of boarding school education on boys and masculinity.

Great fun to read, but biological is B. Greenstein's *The Fragile Male*. 1993. Boxtree.

H. Goldberg. *The Hazards of Being Male*. 1976. NY, Nash.

D. Dinnerstein. *The Mermaid and the Minotaur*. 1976. NY, Harper Row.

2 Attachment, Intimacy, Separation Anxiety and the Fear of Women

1. J. Chasseguet-Smirgel. *Creativity and Perversion*. 1996. Free Association Books.
2. D.W. Winnnicott. 'Fear of breakdown'. 1974. *Int. R. Psycho-Anal.* 1:103–107.
3. See, for example, S. Horley. *The Charm Syndrome*. 1991. Macmillan.
4. J. Gilligan. *Violence. Reflections on our Deadliest Epidemic*. 1996. NY, Putnam.

3 The Fault – Its Origins and Nature

1. S. Freud. *The Dissolution of the Oedipus Complex*. 1925. Standard Edition (hereafter S.E.) 19, p. 173f.
2. See, for example, D. Fuss. *Essentially Speaking*. 1989. Routledge.

3. S. Freud. *The Psychopathology of Everyday Life.* 1901. S.E. 6.
4. S. Freud. *Letters to Fleiss.* 1954. Basic Books.
5. S. Freud. *Outline of Psychoanalysis.* 1938. S.E. 23.
6. See, for example, R. Greenson. 'Disidentifying from mother: its special importance for the boy'. 1968. *Int. J. Psy-Anal.* 49.
7. M. Klein. *Envy and Gratitude and Other Works.* 1975. Hogarth.
8. R.J. Stoller. *Perversion. The Erotic Form of Hatred.* 1975. Maresfield.
9. J. Lacan. *The Four Fundamental Concepts of Psychoanalysis.* 1977. Hogarth.
10. J. Laplanche and J.-B. Pontalis. *The Language of Psychoanalysis.* 1967. Norton.
11. See S. Freud. *The Negative Oedipus Complex.* 1924. S.E. 19.
12. See M. Foucault. *The History of Sexuality.* 1979. Allen Lane.

4 Attachment and Masculinity

1. A simple and accessible summary is provided in J. Bowlby's *A Secure Base.* 1988. Routledge.
2. J. Bowlby. *Attachment and Loss.* 3 vols: *Attachment* (1969); *Separation: Anxiety and Anger* (1972); *Loss: Sadness and Depression* (1980).
3. K. Bartholomew and L. Horowitz. 'Attachment style among young adults'. 1991. *J. Pers. & Soc. Psy.* 61.
4. L.M. Horowitz, S.E. Rosenberg and K. Bartholomew. 'Interpersonal problems, attachment styles, and outcome in brief psychotherapy'. 1993. *J. Cons. and Cl. Psy.* 61:549–560. I am grateful to Kim Bartholomew for her permission to quote freely from her work. I have taken her at her word in what follows.
5. Ibid., p. 554. From 1987 on, C. Hazen and P. Shaver produced a series of brilliant papers on romantic attachment. See especially: 'Romantic love conceptualised as an attachment process'. 1987. *J. Pers. Soc. Psy.* 52. Also see: M. Main and J. Solomon. 1986. In Greenberg et al. *Attachment in Pre-school Years.* University of Chicago.
6. D. Griffin and K. Bartholomew. 'Models of self and other...'. 1994. *J. Int. Rel and Group Proc.* 67. See also: K. Bartholomew and D. Griffin. 'Avoidance of intimacy. An attachment perspective'. 1990. *J. Soc. Pers. Rel.* 7.
7. T. Harris. *I'm OK, You're OK.* 1969. Harper and Row.
8. Bowlby. *A Secure Base.*
9. K. Bartholomew. 'Adult attachment processes: Individual and couple perspectives'. 1997. *Brit. J. Med. Psy.* 70:249–263.

10. K. Bartholomew and L.M. Horowitz. 'Attachment styles among young adults: A test of a four category model'. 1991. *J. Pers. Soc. Psy.* 61:226–244.

5 Sulking, Masculinity and Attachment

1. M. Klein. 'A contribution to the psycho-genesis of manic depressive states'. 1935. *Int. J. Psy-Anal.* 16.
2. J. Masson. *The Assault on Truth*. 1984. Faber and Faber.
3. See J. Gilligan. *Violence. Reflections on our Deadliest Epidemic*. 1996. NY, Putnam.
4. M. Schatzman. *Soul Murder*. 1973. Allen Lane.
5. D. Malan. *The Frontiers of Brief Psychotherapy*. 1979. NY, Plenum.

6 The Domino Theory

1. J. Gilligan. *Violence. Reflections on our Deadliest Epidemic*. 1996. NY, Putnam.
2. M. Schatzman. *Soul Murder*. 1973. Allen Lane.
3. Some authors focus on insecure attachment and spousal abuse and identify this as a major cause. See, for example: D. Dutton and D. Sonkin. 'Treating assaultive men from an attachment perspective'. In *Intimate Violence*. 2003. NY, Haworth.

8 The Use of an Object

1. D.W. Winnicott. 'The use of an object and relating through identifications'. 1969. *Int. J. Psy-Anal.* 50:711–716.
2. O. Kernberg. *Borderline Conditions and Pathologica Narcissism*. 2000. Jason Aronson.
3. R.J. Stoller. *Perversion. The Erotic Form of Hatred*. 1975. Maresfield.
4. Quoted from D. Carveth. 'Dark epiphany: the encounter with finitude or the discovery of the object in the body'. 1994. *Psychoanal. & Contemp. Thought* 17.

9 Phallic Narcissism Re-visited

1. J. Laplanche and J.-B. Pontalis. *The Language of Psychoanalysis*.1967. Norton. p. 309.

2. S. Freud. S.E. 19, 173–179.
3. K. Horney. 'The denial of the vagina'. 1933. *Int. J. Psy-Anal.* 14.
   A. Lampl de Groot. 'The evolution of the Oedipus complex in women'.
   1928. *Int. J. Psy-Anal.* 9.
4. See I. Suttie. *The Origins of Love and Hate.* 1999. Free Association
   Books.
5. Alain de Botton. *Status Anxiety.* 2004. Pantheon.

10   Shame and Perversion

1. M. Main and J. Solomon. 1986. In Greenberg et al. *Attachment in
   Pre-school Years.* University of Chicago.
2. See, for example, J. Cassidy and P.R. Shaver. *The Handbook of
   Attachment,* chapter 23. 1999. Guildford Press.
3. R.J. Stoller. *Sex and Gender. The Development of Masculinity and
   Femininity.* 1984. Maresfield reprint.
4. R. Elkins. *Male Femaling.* 1997. Routledge.

11   Normal Hyper-masculinity

1. D. Malan. *Individual Psychotherapy and the Science of Psychodynamics.*
   1978. Hodder Arnold.
2. Estela Welldon does not agree with this. She believes that the scale
   of mothers' hidden abuse of their children is massive. See *Mother,
   Madonna, Whore.* 1988. Free Association Books.
3. J. Gilligan. *Violence. Reflections on our Deadliest Epidemic.* 1996.
   NY, Putnam.
4. Malan. *Individual Psychotherapy and the Science of Psychodynamics.*
5. F. de Zulueta. *From Pain to Violence.* 2006. Whurr.

12   The Function of Drama

1. E. Berne. *Games People Play.* 1964. Grove Press.
2. A. Bateman, D. Brown and J. Pedder. *Introduction to Psychotherapy.*
   1979. Tavistock Publications.
3. J. Laplanche and J.-B. Pontalis. *The Language of Psychoanalysis.* 1967.
   Norton. p. 17.

4. R. Hinchelwood and W. Skogstad. *Observing Organisations.* 2000. Taylor and Francis.
5. R.J. Stoller. *Perversion. The Erotic Form of Hatred.* 1975. Maresfield.
6. A. Roy. *The God of Small Things.* 1997. Flamingo.

13 The Mad Hypothesis

1. S. Freud. S.E. 9. pp. 231–232.
2. P. Watzlawick, J. Weakland and R. Fisch. *Change. Principles of Problem Formation and Resolution.* 1974. W. Norton and Co.

14 Conclusion

1. A. Phillips. *Monogamy.* 1996. Faber and Faber.

Index

Compiled by Sue Carlton